THE

Importance

OF

Being Foolish

How to Think Like Jesus

BRENNAN MANNING

HarperSanFrancisco
A Division of HarperCollins*Publishers*

HarperCollins books may be purchased for educational, business, or sales promotional use. For information please write: Special Markets Department, HarperCollins Publishers, 10 East 53rd Street, New York, NY 10022.

HarperCollins Web site: http://www.harpercollins.com

HarperCollins®, 🐦®, and HarperSanFrancisco™ are trademarks of HarperCollins Publishers.

FIRST EDITION

Library of Congress Cataloging-in-Publication Data
Manning, Brennan.
The importance of being foolish : how to think like Jesus / Brennan Manning. — 1st ed.
p. cm.
Includes bibliographical references (p.).
ISBN-13: 978–0–06–075165–4
ISBN-10: 0-06-075165–7
1. Christian life—Catholic authors. I. Title.
BX2350.3M26 2005
248.4'82—dc22 2005040317

05 06 07 08 09 RRD(H) 10 9 8 7 6 5 4 3 2 1

Contents

Part Three: The Power of the Cross

Acknowledgments

It is hard to give up on one's children. In 1976, Dimension Books released *Gentle Revolutionaries: Breaking Through to Christian Maturity*. Filled with passion and conviction, I wanted to show how the Church was missing the central points about Jesus's good news to us. Recently, as I came across this abondoned child (since this book went out of print), I discoverd that this message is still an important one for the Church to hear. At the same time, I think I have learned to say things with a little bit more grace and humility than I did in my younger days. So with the help of Carla Barnhill and my friends at HarperSanFrancisco, especially Cindy DiTiberio, I have revised, updated, and fiddled with this earlier work so that now it is ready for, I hope, a new generation of readers. And so for those who have eyes to see and ears to hear, please read on.

Introduction

"It is wonderful what a simple White House invitation will do to dull the critical faculties," warned the late Reinhold Niebuhr. A weighty admonition! The privilege of preaching to the president is so vaunted that most clergymen use the opportunity to repay the compliment. In an atmosphere of mutual admiration, religion dissolves into verbal Alka-Seltzer, and prophetic preaching becomes virtually impossible.

The request from other Christians to write a book on the mind of Jesus has similar, though far less sophisticated, snares. Wanting to please everybody, I am sorely tempted to pen something bland, a treatise riddled with clichés, tortured metaphors, and meaningless stories. Then everybody will be happy and gloriously self-contented. But this book is written out of the conviction that Jesus Christ lived and died and rose in order to form the Holy People of God—a community of Christians who would live under the sway of the Spirit, men and women who would be human torches aglow with the fire of love for Christ, prophets and lovers ignited with the flaming Spirit of the living God. To offer an innocuous effort would be a prostitution of the gospel, an insult to God, and a grave disservice to the reader.

For two years it was my privilege to live with a Christian community known as the Little Brothers of Jesus and to see the theme of this book develop in the undramatic chores of the workaday world. The life of a Little Brother is modeled on the hidden life of Jesus of Nazareth, the many years he spent in obscurity devoted to manual labor and prayer before embarking on his public ministry of preaching, teaching, and healing.

I spent the first six months in the little village of Saint-Remy, France, one hundred-odd miles southeast of Paris. It was a winter of shoveling manure on nearby farms and washing dishes in a local restaurant. The evenings were wrapped in silence in Eucharistic adoration and meditation on the Scriptures. The days passed in a regular rhythm of engagement with and withdrawal from the world. It was a gradual initiation into an uncloistered contemplative life among the poor.

Our group of seven (two Frenchmen, one German, a Spaniard, a Slav, a Korean, and myself) then moved on to Farlete, another small village, in the Zaragosa Desert of Spain. In the twelve months we lived there we came to love the warmth, simplicity, and intimate friendship of a remote Spanish pueblo with a population of six hundred. In summer we worked ten to twelve hours a day in the wheat harvest or on construction jobs, traded turns as cook in the fraternity, and saved enough money to buy six bottles of beer for the Assumption Fiesta, which marked the end of the harvest. Our rapport with the villagers was profound because we shared not only their poverty, toil, bitter bread, and anxiety over the harvest but the joy of a newborn baby, the nuptial bliss of newlyweds, and the multitude of lesser experiences woven into the warp and woof of rural peasant life.

During the year we frequently sojourned in solitude to a high, rocky mountain retreat that is not only far removed from urban life but one of the most remote hermitages in Europe. In many long hours of prayer in the caves, I realized anew that the saving knowledge of Jesus Christ supersedes all else, allowing us to experience a freedom that is not limited by the borders of a world that is itself in chains. At the same time, I recognized that many of the burning theological issues in the church today are neither burning nor theological and that in an age characterized (in some quarters) by confusion, third-rate theatrics, and infidelity, it is not more rhetoric that Jesus demands but personal renewal, fidelity to the gospel, and creative conduct. As Émile Cardinal Leger said in his farewell to Montreal, "The time for talking is over."

This is the fundamental premise around which the 230 disciples who compose the Little Brothers of Jesus have organized their lives. The Little Brothers learn to disentangle essentials from nonessentials and to realize that this particular way of life is simply an exterior consequence of an immense, passionate, and uncompromising love for the person of Jesus. To live among the poorest and most abandoned of peoples as a manual laborer without clerical garb, to pass days and weeks in the desert in the gratuitous praise of God, to communicate through friendship values that cannot be communicated through preaching, satisfies not a desire for novelty but a compulsion of love. Some may call it foolish. I call it true wisdom from the God of Love.

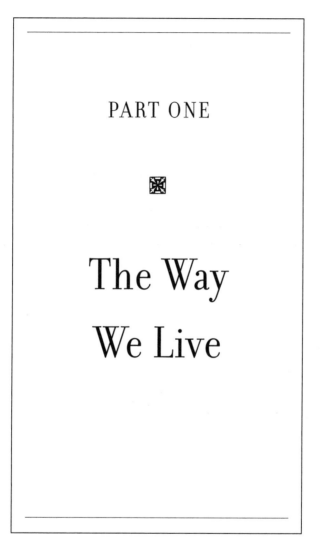

PART ONE

The Way
We Live

1.

Truth

The gospel narrative of the cleans-ing of the temple is a disconcerting scene (John 2:13–22). It presents us with the portrait of an angry Savior. The meek Lamb of God who said, "Take my yoke upon you, and learn from me; for I am gentle and humble of heart" (Matthew 11:29), has fashioned a homemade whip and begun tearing through the temple, overturning stalls and showcases, thrashing the merchants and roaring, "Get out of here! This isn't Wal-Mart. You will not turn sacred space into a shopping excursion! You liars! To visit the temple is a sign of reverence for my Father. Get out of here!"

What is even more disconcerting is Jesus's relentless passion for the truth. In our society, where money, power, and pleasure are the name of the game, the body of truth is bleeding from a thousand wounds. Many of us have been lying to ourselves for so long that our comforting illusions and rationalizations have assumed a patina of truth; we clutch them to our hearts the way a child clutches a favorite teddy bear. Not convinced? Consider the man on his third luncheon martini quoting the Apostle Paul about a little wine being good for the stomach; or the "liberated" Christian's vehement defense of the nudity in *The Last Tango in Paris*, the violence in *Pulp Fiction*, or the oral sex scene in *My Private Idaho*, because they are "integral to the plot and tastefully done"; or the upstanding church deacon who overlooks cheating and manipulation in his business dealings because "it's the only way to be competitive"; or whole churches in which the delirium of guiltlessness is reality, the mastery of biblical exegesis is holiness, the size of the congregation is proof of its authenticity, and on and on. There is no limit to the defenses we contrive against the inbreak of truth into our lives.

The painful question we face in the church today is whether the love of God can be purchased so cheaply. The first step in the pursuit of truth is not the moral resolution to avoid the habit of petty lying—however unattractive a character disfigurement that may be. It is not the decision to stop deceiving others. It is the decision to stop deceiving ourselves. Unless we have the same relentless passion for the truth that Jesus exhibited in the temple, we are undermining our faith, betraying the Lord, and deceiving ourselves. Self-deception is the enemy of wholeness because it prevents us from seeing ourselves as we really are. It covers up our lack of growth in the Spirit of the truthful One and keeps us from coming to terms with our real personalities.

Many years ago I witnessed the power of self-deception dramatically reenacted in the alcoholic rehabilitation center of a small American town. The scene (which is excerpted from my earlier work *The Ragamuffin Gospel*): A large, split-level living room set on the brow of a hill overlooking an artificial lake. Twenty-five men, all chemically dependent on alcohol or drugs, have gathered. Croesus O'Connor, a recovering alcoholic, is the head honcho—a trained counselor, skilled therapist, and senior member of the staff. He summons Max, a small, diminutive man, to sit alone in the center of the U-shaped group. Max is a nominal Christian, married with five children, owner and president of his own company, wealthy and affable, gifted with a remarkable poise. O'Connor begins the interrogation:

"How long you been drinking like a pig, Max?"

Max winces. "That's not quite fair."

"We'll see. Let's get into your drinking history. How much per day?"

"Well, I have two Marys with the men before lunch and two Martins when the office closes at five. Then. . . ."

"What in God's name are Marys and Martins?" Croesus interrupts.

"Bloody Marys—vodka, tomato juice, a dash of Worcestershire—and Martinis—extra dry, straight up, ice cold, with an olive and lemon twist."

"Thank you, Mary Martin. Go on."

"The wife likes a drink before dinner. Got her hooked on Martins years back." Max smiles. "You understand that, right, guys?" No one responds. "We have two then and two before bed."

"Eight drinks a day, Max?" Croesus inquires.

"That's right. Not a drop more, not a drop less."

"You're a liar!"

Max is not ruffled. "I'll pretend I didn't hear that. Been in business twenty-eight years. People know my word is my bond. Built my reputation on veracity, not mendacity."

"Ever hide a bottle in your house?" asks Benjamin, a Native American from New Mexico.

"Don't be ridiculous. Got a bar in my living room as big as a horse's ass. Nothing personal, Mr. O'Connor." Mary Martin is smiling again.

"Do you keep any booze in the garage, Mary?"

"Naturally. Got to replenish the stock. I do a lot of home entertaining in my business. You understand that, right, guys?" No response.

"How many bottles in the garage?"

"I really don't know. Offhand I'd say two cases of vodka, four cases of gin, and a bevy of liqueurs."

The interrogation continues another twenty minutes. Max dodges, ducks, evades, hedges, fudges, minimizes, rationalizes, and justifies his drinking pattern. Finally, hemmed in by relentless cross-examination, he reluctantly admits that he keeps a bottle in the nightstand, one in a suitcase for travel purposes, another in his bathroom cabinet for medicinal purposes, and three more at the office for entertaining clients. He squirms occasionally but never loses his veneer of confidence or serene sense of self-possession.

"You're a liar!" another voice booms.

"No need to get vindictive, Charlie," Max shoots back. "Remember the biblical image in John's Gospel about the speck in your brother's eye and the two-by-four in your own? And the other one, Matthew this time, about the pot and the kettle."

O'Connor picks up the phone and dials a number in a distant city. It is Max's hometown. O'Connor puts the call on speakerphone. A man answers.

"Hank Shea?" asks O'Connor.

"Yeah, who's this?"

"My name is Croesus O'Connor. I'm a counselor at a rehabilitation center in the Midwest, and I need some help. You remember a customer named Max?"

"Yep," comes the reply.

"Good. With his family's permission, I'm researching his drinking history. You tend bar in that establishment every afternoon, so I was wondering if you could tell me roughly how much Max drinks each day."

"I know Max, but you sure you got his okay to do this?"

"I got a signed affidavit. Shoot."

"He's a helluva guy. I really like him. He drops a hundred bucks in here every afternoon. Has eight martinis, buys a few drinks, and always leaves me a big tip. Good man."

Max leaps to his feet and lets loose with a stream of profanity. He attacks O'Connor's ancestry, assails Charlie's legitimacy, and impugns the whole unit's integrity. He bellows, bleats, and blasphemes. He claws at the sofa and spits on the rug.

Then he regains his composure. He reseats himself, readjusts his mask, realigns his defenses, and remarks matter-of-factly that even Jesus lost his cool in the temple when he saw the "Sadoocees" hawking pigeons and pastries. After an extemporaneous homily to the group on justifiable anger, he sits back and presumes that the inquiry is over.

"Have you ever been unkind to one of your kids?" Fred Bedloe asks.

"Glad you brought that up, Fred. I've got a fantastic rapport with my four boys. Last Thanksgiving I took them on a fishing expedition to the Rockies. Four days of roughing it in the wilderness. Helluva time! Two graduated from Harvard, you know, and Max Junior is in his third year at . . . "

"I didn't ask you that. At least once in his life every father has been unkind to one of his kids. I'm sixty-two and can vouch for it. Now give us one specific example."

A long pause ensues. Finally, Max responds, "Well, I was a little unkind to my nine-year-old daughter last Christmas Eve."

"What happened?"

"Don't remember. Just get this heavy feeling whenever I think about it."

"Where did it happen? What were the circumstances?"

"Wait one damn minute!" Max says, his anger rising again. "I told you I don't remember. Just have this bad feeling."

Unobtrusively, O'Connor dials Max's hometown once more and speaks with Max's wife.

"Croesus O'Connor calling, ma'am. Your husband just told me he was unkind to your daughter last Christmas Eve. Can you give me the details, please?"

A soft voice fills the room. "Yes, I can tell you. Our daughter, Debbie, wanted a certain pair of shoes for Christmas. On the afternoon of the twenty-fourth, my husband drove her downtown, gave her forty dollars, and told her to buy whatever she wanted. That's what she did. When she got back in the truck, she kissed Max and told him he was the best daddy in the whole world. He was probably preening himself like a peacock and decided to celebrate on the way home. He stopped at a tavern near here and told Debbie he'd be right out. It was a cold clear day, about eighteen degrees, so Max left the motor running and locked both doors so no one could get in. It was a little after three in the afternoon and . . . "

Silence.

"Yes?"

The sound of heavy breathing. Her voice grows faint. She is fighting back tears. "My husband came out of the bar at midnight. He was drunk. The motor had stopped, and the windows were frozen shut. Debbie was badly frostbitten on both ears and her fingers. When we got her to the hospital, the doctors had to operate. They amputated the thumb and forefinger in her right hand. She'll be deaf the rest of her life."

Max looks like he is having a seizure. He is on his feet making short, jerky, uncoordinated movements. His glasses fly from his face as he collapses on all fours and begins sobbing hysterically.

O'Connor stands up and says quietly, "Let's go." As the men get up to leave, they look at Max. None of them will forget what they see: Mary Martin, urbane, wealthy, sophisticated man of the world, father of five, chronic alcoholic, is still on all fours. His sobs have soared to shrieks. O'Connor approaches him, pushes his foot against Max's rib cage so that he rolls over on his back.

"Look, pig, there's the door and there's the window. Take whichever one you can get out of fastest. I'm not running a hotel for liars!"

If this sounds like a brutal response, keep in mind that this rehabilitation center's philosophy of tough love is based on the conviction, born of long experience, that no effective recovery can be initiated until a person admits that he is powerless over alcohol and that his life has become unmanageable. The alternative to confronting the truth of his situation is always some form of self-destruction. For Max there were three options—eventual insanity, premature death, or abstinence. However, no choice was possible until the enemy was identified through a painful, merciless interaction with his peers. His self-deception had to be unmasked in all its absurdity.

The sequel to this story is interesting. Max pleaded for and obtained permission to stay. He then proceeded to undergo the most striking personality transformation the group had ever witnessed. He became honest and more sincere, more open, more affectionate, and more vulnerable than he had been before. Tough love made him real, and the truth set him free.

The denouement to his story is even more interesting. The night before Max completed treatment, another man, Fred, passed by his room. The door was ajar. Max was sitting at his desk reading the novel *Watership Down*. Fred knocked and greeted him. For several minutes Max sat staring at the book. When he looked up, his cheeks were streaked with tears. "Fred," he said hoarsely, "I just prayed for the first time in my life."

In his autobiography, Saint Augustine showed the close connection between the quest for truth and conversion of heart. Max could not encounter the truth of the living God until he faced the reality of his alcoholism. From a biblical perspective, Max was a liar. In philosophy, the opposite of truth is error; in Scripture, the opposite of truth is a lie. Max's lie consisted of giving the appearance of existence to what did not exist— harmless social drinking. Truth for him consisted in detaching himself from appearances in order to acknowledge reality—his alcoholism.

In John's Gospel, the liar stubbornly blinds himself to light and truth and plunges into darkness. The devil is the father of lies: "He was a murderer from the beginning, not holding to the truth, for there is no truth in him. When he lies, he speaks his native language, for he is a liar and the father of lies" (John 8:44). The devil is the great illusionist. He varnishes the truth. "If we claim to be without sin, we deceive ourselves and the truth is not in us" (1 John 1:8). He prompts us to give importance to what has no importance; he clothes with a false glitter what is least substantial and turns us away from what is surpassingly real. He causes us to live in a world of delusion, unreality, and shadows.

The conflict between the father of lies and the truth who is Jesus Christ dominates John's Gospel. The Lord has not only vanquished the liar but given us a share in his victory through the Holy Spirit; the exaltation of Jesus Christ on the Cross releases the Spirit. The paschal triumph has not only expiated our sins and justified us before God but brought the outpouring of the Holy Spirit who has been given to us (Romans 5:5). The Spirit enables us to conquer lying, self-deception, and dishonesty, endears us to the truth of God, and leads us to savor eternal realities.

The late Jean Daniélou wrote, "Truth consists in the mind's giving to things the importance they have in reality." What is truly real to the believer is God. When Max was driven to confront and accept the truth of his alcoholism, he stepped through a doorway into the acknowledgment of God's sovereign reality and claimed, "I just prayed for the first time in my life."

The implications here for the serious Christian seeking to have the mind of Christ Jesus (Philippians 2:5) and the fullness of life in the Holy Spirit are far-reaching. For the majority of us, what is most real is the world of our material existence; what is most unreal is the world of God. This is a fact so enormous, a subversion so radical, that the liar in the biblical sense is largely taken for granted in our society. For the religious dimension of life is a kind of optional accessory, entirely a matter of taste. Faith is a halfhearted assent to a dusty pawnshop collection of dogmatic declarations. What's needed in this world are people of influence, people who move and shake with the best of them, people who stand on their own two feet and direct their own destinies. It is the powerful who get things done, not those who stand in brokenness and need.

Those, you might say, are the motives of the godless; we are different. We believe in religion, in faith. Perhaps. Yet there is a breed of liars who are open to the Spirit of Jesus but in a superficial fashion. They receive everything, but nothing remains rooted. They champion ecclesial renewal and change for change's sake. They spot the speck of sawdust in the hierarchical eye but not the two-by-four in their own. They are pro-life where the unborn fetus is concerned but anti-life where the Muslim, the sinful, and the guilty are concerned. Butterfly types who sip on a thousand different blossom cups. Sanguine people of the moment—today elated to the heavens, tomorrow depressed to the point of death. They guide themselves by what's new and swim with the stream. Their highest moral imperative is to keep up a good front. Never suggest to them that the cost of discipleship is high, that there is no cheap Pentecost. Weathervane Christians who cannot be trusted, their number is legion.

However, our concern in these pages is the sincere Christian whose faith is firm and rooted. Jesus Christ is (or is on the way to becoming) the most important person in her life. Her prayer is neither pretense nor facade. She is intelligent in the biblical sense, and she knows reality as it is. In the Scriptures intelligence does not consist in the more or less brilliant performance of the mind. It consists in recognizing the omnipresent reality of God. "The fool says in his heart: 'There is no God'" (Psalm 14:1). From the biblical perspective, a great theologian may be stupid; an illiterate washerwoman praising God for the sunset immeasurably more intelligent. The Christian spoken to in these pages, whatever her station or status in life, is presumed to be intelligent and interested in the pursuit of truth.

The Loss of Wonder

On a cold night brilliant with starshine, I stood on the edge of darkness awaiting the sunrise. The desert sands gleamed like silvered sugar. Over and over the wind whispered his name to me, "Abba, Abba." The vigil was ended, and my life would never be the same. In a solitary cave in the Zaragosa wilderness, I came to *know* God as my Father. I was a child again lost in wonder, love, and praise.

To become a little child again (as Jesus enjoined we must) is to recapture a sense of surprise, wonder, and vast delight in all of reality. Look at a child's face on Christmas morning as he enters the living room transformed by the midnight passage of Santa Claus. Or when he discovers the coin under the pillow or sees his first rainbow or sniffs his first rose. Few of us catch our breath at these things as we once did. The walk down the corridor of time has made us bigger and everything else smaller, less impressive.

We know our strength of mind and will. We have acquired a certain mastery over nature, over illness. Through the miracle of modern technology we are able to experience sights, sounds, and happenings once available only to Columbus, Balboa, and other adventurers. There was a time in the not-too-distant past when a thunderstorm caused grown men to shudder and feel small. But God is being edged out of his world by science. The more man knows about meteorology, the less inclined he is to make the sign of the Cross during a thunderstorm. Airplanes now fly above, below, and around entire storm systems. Satellites reduce these once-terrifying events to photographs. What ignominy (if a thunderstorm could experience ignominy) to be reduced from theophany to nuisance!

Even outer space has gradually ceased to impress us. We talk about probes on Mars with the same excitement as if we had sent cameras to the East Village in

New York. We have become jaded, incapable of wonder and awe. This lessening of impressionability may be a sign of maturity, a necessary and healthy consequence of progress. But I tend to think it betrays a loss of equilibrium. A truly balanced person retains a capacity for wonder and the willingness to express it in the very confession of creaturehood, the spontaneous acknowledgment that he is a human being and not a god, a being with limitations who, far from having embraced infinity, is happily and hopelessly engulfed by it.

Our laconic response to reality is even more somnolent when we encounter Jesus Christ and explore the Christian way of life. Though confronted with an ethic so sublime and so demanding that it seems utterly impossible, we are not stupefied by the lifestyle that Christ has set before us. He says that the standard for the Christian way of life is *agape*. "Greater love has no one than this, that he lay down his life for his friends" (John 15:13). In Pauline locution, the love of Jesus is a *kenosis*, a total self-emptying. And Christ categorically says: "As I have loved you, so you must love one another" (John 13:34). Though he proposes an intensity of goodness and holiness before which we can only whisper, "Who then can be saved?" there remains an awesome absence of amazement. We resemble the sprinter asked to run the 100-meter in five seconds. After several futile attempts, he becomes upset over the condition of the track and complains about the pinch in his shoes. The fact that the project is humanly impossible never strikes him.

We must take the time to gape a while at what is asked of us. Ponder just a few of the radical demands recorded in the synoptic Gospels:

If someone strikes you on the right cheek, turn to him the other also. (Matthew 5:39)

If someone wants to sue you and take your tunic, let him have your cloak as well. (Matthew 5:40)

Give to the one who asks you, and do not turn away from the one who wants to borrow from you. (Matthew 5:42)

In these passages, Jesus describes the Christian's response when he is acted on by another. But his teachings are not merely passive: "Love your enemies [even Saddam Hussein], and pray for those who persecute you" (Matthew 5:44).

Jesus presents his heavenly Father as our model. As God rains peace and goodness on the just and unjust alike, so should we. Anyone can love their friends, those with whom we have a mutuality, a reciprocity. True godliness demands much, much more.

The Sermon on the Mount continues:

If your right eye causes you to sin, gouge it out and throw it away. (Matthew 5: 29)

If your right hand causes you to sin, cut it off and throw it away. (Matthew 5:30)

When the call of Christ comes, our response must be wholehearted: "Lord, first let me go and bury my father," asks the disciple. "But Jesus said, 'Follow me, and let the dead bury their own dead'" (Matthew 8:21–22).

The renouncement—utter renouncement—of family is involved: "If anyone comes to me and does not hate his father and mother, his wife and children, his brothers and sister—yes, even his own life—he cannot be my disciple" (Luke 14:25–26).

Jesus says:

Blessed are you when people insult you, persecute you, and falsely say all kinds of evil against you because of me. Rejoice and be glad because great is your reward in heaven. (Matthew 5:11–12)

Do not suppose that I have come to bring peace to the earth. I did not come to bring peace, but a sword. (Matthew 10:34)

If the world hates you, keep in mind that it hated me first. (John 15:18)

On and on they go. Extravagant, overstated assertions. The Christ of God has not come to bring peace but the sword; he would have us put on not dressing gowns but the armor of God. He contradicts our conclusion that prose is poetry, speech is song, myopia is clear vision, that what's tangible, visible, and perishable can be adequate achievement for a being who has inhaled the creative thrust of God.

The only sane reaction to the evangelical standard of holiness is awe and confusion bordering on complaint. We should be embarrassed by the Word because it says much that we don't want to hear. But why are most of us not embarrassed? Why doesn't the Word exalt, frighten, and shock us? It's not because we are unfamiliar with it—we hear it week in and week out. Why doesn't it force us to reassess our lives?

It comes back to our delusions. Michel Quoist says:

> *We are satisfied by our decent little life. We are*
> *pleased with our good habits; we take them for virtues.*
> *We are pleased with our little efforts; we take them*
> *for progress. We are proud of our activities; they*
> *make us think we are giving ourselves. We are*
> *impressed by our influence; we imagine that it will*
> *transform lives. We are proud of what we give,*
> *though it hides what we withhold. We may even*
> *be mistaking a set of coinciding egoisms for real*
> *friendship.*

As the sincere Christian opens himself to the life proposed by Jesus—a life of constant prayer and total unselfishness, a life of buoyant, creative goodness and a purity of heart that goes beyond chastity to affect every facet of our personality—his sense of awe and wonder can quickly sour into cynicism and pessimism. The suspicion grows that the gospel ethic is impractical, impossible, and therefore irrelevant. The words are nice, but who pays them any mind? After all, I can't be asked to do all that! I can't survive in the jungle out there if I take Jesus's revelation seriously. I can't be always giving. There must be a limit. But Christ sets no limits.

This is the real problem that must be faced. Is the gospel ethic outdated and irrelevant? Does anyone pay attention to it? Should we try to avoid it in our teaching? In the course of history, several solutions have been proposed to defuse the dynamite in Jesus's moral teaching. According to one approach, "Jesus is coming from an Eastern perspective. You know how they tend to focus on mysticism. They're not rationalists like us." We have projected our staid, Western mentality on the poetic, creative, Semitic thought patterns of Jesus. After all, no man has a beam in his eye! And then that impossible image: "It is easier for a camel to pass through the eye of a needle than for a rich man to enter the kingdom of God." Such language is more than impossible. It's ignorant! Aren't we determined by economics? Money rules the world. Even Christian undertakings must be financed. And then those images of the pains of the woman in labor, as found in John, and the emptying of the bowels, as found in Mark. The language is too strong. The people won't understand. It is more prudent to render these dangerous maxims harmless. Pour as much water as possible into the fiery wine of Christ. After all, he was Eastern.

Very well. Let's grant that. Nonetheless, Jesus said: "Forgive your neighbor seventy times seven times" (Matthew 18:22). Even if this admonition is an "Eastern exaggeration," it means something. And what is the meaning of the many other keen formulations that Jesus loved so much? What is the sense of that pregnant sentence "the good news is preached to the poor" (Matthew 11:5)? One wonders how many of those railing against the presence of Christians in antiwar demonstrations have been educated to the truth that the church's mission is to preach the gospel to the poor. How many religious orders, which were founded to teach the poor, are now so expensive that the poor cannot afford them? Do we dismiss the text "Forgive your neighbor seventy times seven times" as an Eastern exaggeration, or are we forced to admit that the sign of Christ's church is that it is to be the privileged place of the poor? Isn't the Messiah to be recognized through his ministry to the poor? "Are you the Messiah," the disciples ask John the Baptist, "or are we to wait for some other?" (see Luke 3:15). Jesus says to the people, "Go and report to

John what you have seen and heard: the blind receive sight, the lame walk, those who have leprosy are cured, the deaf hear, the dead are raised, and the good news is preached to the poor" (Luke 7:22).

The church in all its structures must be a sign of Christ's love raised up to the poor. In passing over this painful sentence, the church itself has become poor, as well as too unsure and unconvinced to preach the gospel with clarity and vision, and too childishly attached to the bric-a-brac of honors, the double-talk of diplomacy, the degrading favors of the rich, the idolatry of structures, and the price of place.

A second theory holds that Jesus is proposing principles as opposed to rules. He isn't talking about practical applications. He is simply proposing a goal, an idealistic picture toward which we should strive. This reduces Christ to the level of a romantic visionary: his teaching is beautiful in theory but impractical in fact. Certainly if his gospel were lived there would be no international wars, no national upheavals or domestic disputes. But Christ was simply a starry-eyed reformer with a lot of grandiose ideas.

Then there is the second-class citizenship solution. This view maintains that the ethical teaching of Jesus was intended only for a particular class. There are two classes of citizenship in the Kingdom of God, the perfect and the ordinary. The latter are not called to perfection. Yet the Sermon on the Mount emphatically proclaims the universal vocation of all Christians to holiness. There are no distinctions between the "holy" and the common.

In truth, these reasons for rejecting the way of Jesus are more palatable than the one that many Christians choose: the gospel ethic is too disturbing, too problematic to live out. Let us shove it under the rug and forget about it. If you tell it like it is, people will be turned off. We are reluctant to structure our moral teaching around the gospel. For example, in three different places the New Testament tells us quite clearly that our sins are forgiven in proportion to the degree we forgive others. This truth is vividly depicted in the parable of the merciless servant. He owes his master more than ten million dollars, while his fellow servant owes him the comparatively paltry sum of twenty-five dollars. There is a screaming disproportion between the debts. Yet even when his master graciously forgives his debt, the servant will not forgive his debtor. The moral is clear: if we do not forgive our enemies, we ourselves are not forgiven (see Luke 6:37). For a long time the theology of the confession of sins has not been presented in this perspective. We have quibbled over the approximate number of times and the precise species of sin for which forgiveness might be warranted. We consider the boundaries crossed and the equal division of blame. When we do offer forgiveness, we do so too often with a spirit of superiority, using forgiveness as something to hold over the head of those we have deigned to let off the hook.

The New Testament is relevant only if we grasp the fundamental meaning of the radical demands of the gospel while at the same time understanding that we can never completely fulfill them. None of us can say, "I have kept all the commandments." We always fall short to some extent. Think again of forgiveness. In our hearts none of us have completely forgiven our enemies the way we should. In Jesus's post-Resurrection encounter with the apostles on the beach along the Sea of Tiberias, when one might have expected, as Raymond Brown says, "the impact of unbearable glory," Jesus serves fish and chips. There is no mention, apparently even no memory, of their betrayal. Never a reproach or even an indirect reference to their cowardice in the time of testing. No sarcastic greeting like, "Well, my fair-weather friends. . . ." No vindictiveness, spite, or humiliating reproach. Only words of warmth and tenderness. The same in the Upper Room as Jesus says, "*Peace* be to you."

This is more than forgiveness. The silence of Jesus is exquisite. To learn the meaning of steadfast friendship, delicacy in dialogue, sensitivity to the feelings of others, and love that "keeps no record of wrongs" (1 Corinthians 13:5), one must listen to the forgiveness in the heart of Jesus as he says to Mary Magdalene on Easter morning, "Go and tell *my brothers . . .* " (Matthew 28:10).

The demands of the gospel bring us to the vivid awareness of our weakness and imperfection. They stun us, reduce our overestimation of ourselves, and make us realize how limited we are. This realization—when we allow it to infiltrate our hearts—keeps us from smugness, complacency, and the self-sufficiency that poisons spirituality. God's Word wakes us up to our need. Until we submit our lives to the judgment of the gospel and the standards of goodness and virtue established by Jesus, there can be no profound consciousness of being a sinner in need of mercy. How many of us have actually tasted the truth that *we are saved;* that we do not save ourselves; that in very truth we are poor, weak sinners with hereditary faults and limited virtues; that we are God's children not by our merit but by God's mercy.

If the radical demands of the Christian life are never proposed, if we settle instead for the tepid observance of a lukewarm set of precepts, how easily we become pharisaical and self-righteous. We try to save ourselves by our own works. We never experience the mystery of redemption or loving dependence on God. According to our own invulnerable standards of justice and honor, we are doing quite well at playing Christian. How often does a Catholic penitent come to the sacrament of reconciliation and begin: "Bless me, Father, for I have sinned. It has been a year since my last confession. I went to Mass every Sunday and didn't eat meat on the days we weren't supposed to. I can't think of anything else." Such a confession is a terrible reproach to Christian catechesis.

If we wink at the radical demands of the New Testament in our teaching and ignore the embarrassing implications of the precept of universal love, we make Christianity too easy and take away its meaning. We become as guilty as the Pharisees, ignoring the weightier matters of the difficult laws of charity, mercy, and faith while observing the positive laws of the church that are meant only as the boundaries of the Christian commitment.

The radical demands of Jesus daily remind us of our shortcomings and make us realize that salvation is God's free gift. Here we reach the heart of revelation. If the gospel tells us anything, if the church proclaims just one thing year in and year out, it is that salvation is God's free gift. The gospel is the glad tiding of gratuitous redemption. "You are a chosen people, a royal priesthood, a holy nation, a people belonging to God, that you may declare the praises of darkness into his wonderful light. Once you were not a people, but now you are the people of God; once you had not received mercy, but now you have received mercy" (1 Peter 2:9–10). We have been translated into the kingdom of God's beloved Son not by our merit but by his mercy:

> *For it is by grace you have been saved through*
> *faith—and this is not from yourselves, it is the gift of*
> *God—not by works, so that no one can boast. For we*
> *are God's workmanship, created in Christ Jesus to do*

good works, which God prepared in advance for us to do. (Ephesians 2:8–10)

The gospel would have us appreciate once and for all that the Salvation Army slogan "Jesus Saves" is much closer to the mind and heart of Christ than legalizing and moralizing.

The Blessing

This very theme is contained in the first beatitude: "Blessed are the poor in spirit, for theirs is the kingdom of heaven" (Matthew 5:3). In its primitive meaning, the first beatitude was never intended to moralize or to threaten ("detach yourself from money, materiality, and all creature comforts or else"). Nor was the first beatitude meant to be a simple promise of compensation such as any itinerant preacher could have made ("live like a poor man and you will get to heaven"). On the contrary, the beatitude is a glad tiding, the great good news that the messianic era has erupted into history, the proclamation that the long-awaited day of salvation has finally arrived.

The crucial question in determining the original sense of this beatitude is, who are the poor whom Jesus declares blessed? Are we to understand "poor" in a social sense as those who are literally destitute, impoverished, indigent? Or does Jesus use "poor" in a religious sense to refer to those who depend entirely on God for all that they have and who realize their own unworthiness and therefore accept salvation as the gift of God in Christ Jesus?

To understand its real meaning, this text cannot be isolated. Rather, it must be situated within the context of the whole gospel. Jesus announces that the poor have a privileged place in the kingdom. Let us compare the poor of the first beatitude with two other privileged classes in the gospel.

Matthew's Gospel tells us that *children* have a special claim on God's love:

> *At that time the disciples came to Jesus and asked,*
> *"Who is the greatest in the kingdom of heaven?" He*
> *called a little child and had him standing among*
> *them. And he said, "I tell you the truth, unless you*
> *change and become like little children, you will never*
> *enter the kingdom of heaven. Therefore, whoever*
> *humbles himself like this child is the greatest in the*
> *kingdom of heaven." (Matthew 18:1–4)*

There is no mistaking that one must learn to resemble a child in order to enter the kingdom. But to grasp the full force of the phrase "like little children," we must realize that the Jewish attitude toward children in the time of Christ differed drastically from the one prevalent today. We have a tendency to idealize child-hood, to see it as the happy age of innocence, insou-ciance, and simple faith. In the Jewish community of New Testament times, the child was considered of no importance, meriting no attention or favor. The child was regarded with scorn.

For the disciple of Jesus, being like a child means accepting oneself as being of little account, unimpor-tant. This understanding of ourselves changes not only the way we view our worth but also the way we view God's saving grace. If a little Jewish child received a ten-cent allowance from her father at the end of the week, she did not regard it as payment for sweeping the house, doing the dishes, and baking the bread. It was a wholly unmerited gift, a gesture of her father's absolute liberality. Jesus gave these scorned little ones the privi-lege of his kingdom and presented them as models to his disciples. They were to accept the gift of the king-dom in the same way a child accepts his allowance. If the children were privileged, it was not because they had merited privilege, but simply because God took pleasure in them. The mercy of the Lord flowed to them wholly and entirely from unmerited grace and divine preference.

A second important passage highlights the children's privilege. The hymn of jubilation reads, "I praise you, Father, Lord of heaven and earth, because you have hidden these things from the wise and the learned, and revealed them to little children. Yes, Father, for this was your good pleasure" (Luke 10:21).

God's blessing falls on children because they are negligible creatures, not because of their good qualities. They may be aware of their worthlessness, but this is not the reason why revelations are given to them. Jesus expressly attributes the blessing they receive to the Father's good pleasure, the divine *eudokia*. The gifts are not determined by the slightest personal quality or virtue. They are pure liberality.

The beatitude of the little ones then offers an illuminating insight into the meaning of the beatitude of the poor. In the mentality of New Testament times, poverty and childhood were regarded with equal contempt. However, Jesus says that God prefers the underprivileged. God is pleased to give a privileged place in the kingdom to those whom the world considers most unfortunate.

Further light is cast on the first beatitude in a striking way by the *sinners'* privilege. Jesus is seated at table in Levi's house. The Scribes and Pharisees badger Jesus as to why he eats with tax collectors and sinners. "Jesus said to them, 'It is not the healthy who need a doctor, but the sick. I have not come to call the righteous, but sinners'" (Mark 2:17).

The sinners to whom Jesus directed his messianic mission were real sinners. They had done nothing to merit salvation. Yet they opened themselves to the gift that was offered them. The self-righteous, on the other hand, put their trust in what they had merited by their own efforts and closed their hearts to the message of salvation.

But the salvation Jesus promises cannot be earned. There can be no bargaining with God in a petty poker table atmosphere: "I have done this, therefore you owe me that." Jesus utterly destroys the juridical notion that our works demand payment in return. This teaching is clearly set forth in the parable of the laborers in the vineyard. When they learn that those who have worked but one hour are to receive the same wages as those who have worked all day, the laborers complain to the owner:

> "These men who were hired last worked only one
> hour," they said, "and you have made them equal to
> us who have borne the burden of the work and the
> heat of the day." But he answered one of them,
> "Friend, I am not being unfair to you. Didn't you
> agree to work for a denarius? Take your pay and go.
> I want to give the man who was hired last the same as
> I gave you. Don't I have the right to do what I want
> with my own money? Or are you envious because I am
> generous?" (Matthew 20:12–15)

Our puny works do not entitle us to barter with God. Everything depends on God's good pleasure.

The salvation offered by Jesus is purely gratuitous, intended especially for those who have no title to it, those who are so conscious of their unworthiness that they have to rely on the mercy of God. The self-righteous imagine that they have earned salvation through observance of the law. Refusing to give up this madness, they reject the merciful love of the redeeming God.

In the misery of the sinner, Jesus sees the possibility of salvation. "Of such is the kingdom of God." If in Russia the sinner was once sent to Siberia, in the church she is called to the kingdom. It is a pure gift to those who have no right to it. This is the very heart of the gospel and the fundamental theme of the beatitudes—the nonvalue of the beneficiaries of the kingdom. To say that we are ciphers is not to denigrate our dignity but to highlight the absolute gratuity of God's promise.

Thus, the privileged condition of children and sinners sheds considerable light on the primitive meaning of the first beatitude. Blessed are the poor. Blessed are you who are conscious of your lack of merit and readily open yourselves to the divine mercy.

The first beatitude, then, is not a promise or a threat. Jesus joyfully proclaims the dawn of a new era, the messianic age that has come at last. "You poor, you nobodies, you of little account by the world's standards, you are blessed. It is my Father's good pleasure to give you a privileged place in the kingdom—not because you worked so hard, and not because you are saying all the right things or doing all the right things or becoming all the right things, but because my Father wants you."

Poverty of spirit is presented to us as the indispensable disposition for the disciple of Jesus. The moment we stand before God stuttering like the prophet Jeremiah, our feet on the ground, conscious of our smallness and weakness, acknowledging that Jesus saves, then the high holiness commanded by Jesus—"Be perfect, therefore, as your heavenly Father is perfect" (Matthew 5:48)—begins to flower within us. The primary posture of the Christian is a childlike openness to God, and our primary attitude one of thanksgiving.

Such a stance contrasts sharply with the thinking of many Christians who have developed a false sense of security because they observe church laws. John McKenzie writes:

> *Morality spoils their religion. They suffer from a legalistic hangup. They believe that fulfilling the external prescriptions of the law automatically guarantees the fulfillment of the purpose of the law. But if the fact of my adhering to laws (which I may truly need) does not further the final goal of my life, which is to know Christ Jesus and live his gospel, then mere external conformity does very little if anything.*

My personal experience of the Father during my time with the Little Brothers of Jesus did not result in any sudden or dramatic progress in virtue or moral perfection in my life. After that experience, I may not have been any better than before, but in some way life had changed. Everything had been transformed simply because I had accepted the fact that I am accepted. Paul Tillich called this *grace*.

What a significant difference when we bring this understanding to our worship! We are worshipers of the saving love and mercy of the God who has accepted us. We are steeped in gratitude and dependence. Our very being is a Eucharist, a permanent and perpetual thanksgiving to God. The Psalms remind us that whenever God's people are gathered together, an attitude of joyful thanksgiving is the thanks offering of the assembly (Psalms 95:2; 100:4; 147:7). If Eucharist means thanksgiving, Christianity means people who are joyfully thankful people.

The joyful Christian is one who has retained a sense of awe and wonder before God, one who has existentially experienced membership in a redeemed community. She has a lively faith-appreciation of this great gift. She has opened up to the truth that everything she has is from God, that she is completely dependent on Christ, that "Jesus saves." Of course, on a given day she may come to worship more depressed than anything else. In this vale of tears no Christian life is an unbroken, upward spiral to the mountaintop. Yet the Christian's basic orientation is one of joy and gratitude. Such is the legacy of the paschal mystery, the death and resurrection of Jesus. We are God's children not by our merit but by God's mercy.

This is the sign we place at each worship celebration. When the gift of gratuitous redemption is made present under the veil of symbol, the Pauline cry springs spontaneously from the heart: "How rich God is in mercy! With what an excess of love he has loved us" (see Ephesians 2:4).

When the light of this awesome truth bursts upon our consciousness, most of us are deeply moved for a few moments or hours; then we return to the normal occupations of our pedestrian existence without getting unraveled. Not Charles de Foucauld, the priest whose life and ministry would inspire the formation of the Little Brothers of Jesus. It blew his mind. It signaled the dawn of a new life. An immense joy filled his heart, greater than any happiness he had ever known. What makes his life different from ours is that his sense of wonder never disappeared: "As soon as I believed that there was a God, I understood that I could do nothing else than live for him exclusively: my religious vocation dates from the same hour as my faith."

2.

Transparency

To grasp the truth of the gospel is to fall on our faces in both sorrow and gratitude. To live as Jesus lived is to move off the floor and into the world. "The imitation of Jesus Christ," writes George Montague, "goes to the very assimilation of his interior attitudes, his way of thinking." The late Romano Guardini once stated that Francis of Assisi "allowed Jesus Christ to become transparent in his personality." If this is what it means to live as a Christian, why are the personalities of so many pious, proper, and correct Christians so opaque? Why doesn't the peace of Christ Jesus reign in our hearts, "since as members of the one body we have been called to peace"

(Colossians 3:15)? Why don't the gentleness, compassion, and trust that Much Afraid saw shining in the eyes of the Shepherd (in Hannah Hurnard's *Hinds' Feet on High Places*) shine from our eyes? Why don't our contagious joy, enthusiasm, and gratitude infect others with a love for Christ Jesus? Why doesn't the radiant loveliness of the Lord stream from our personalities? Why aren't we windows to God at work? Why aren't we transparent?

To have the mind of Christ Jesus, to think his thoughts, share his ideals, dream his dreams, throb with his desires, replace our natural responses to persons and situations with the concern of Jesus, and make the mind-set of Christ so completely our own that "the life I now live in the body, I live by faith in the Son of God, who loved me and gave himself for me" (Galatians 2:20), is not the secret of or the shortcut to transparency. It *is* transparency.

Often our preoccupation with the three most basic human desires—security, pleasure, and power—is the cloak that covers transparency. The endless struggle for enough money, good feelings, and prestige yields a rich harvest of worry, frustration, suspicion, anger, jealousy, anxiety, fear, and resentment. These powerful, emotion-backed desires cause 99 percent of the self-inflicted and unnecessary suffering in our lives. They continually focus our attention on self and keep us from being transparent, dimming the light and obscuring "the glory of God in the face of Christ" (2 Corinthians 4:6).

John the evangelist speaks of the sinner as being in a state of darkness. "[He] walks around in the darkness; he does not know where he is going, because the darkness has blinded him" (1 John 2:11). It is the ego-dominated self that keeps us locked in a series of competitive moves and countermoves, that induces us to manipulate people and control situations, that for most of us destroys inner peace and serenity in our lives. Trapped in the quest for security, pleasure, and power, our moment-to-moment thoughts are concentrated on the dark pursuit of illusory happiness, and we are thus inattentive to the Lord of Light. Our eyes are not fixed on Christ Jesus but on ourselves. We settle for a roller-coaster ride of exhilarating peaks and vertiginous valleys, interspersed with long periods of driving, pushing, and suffering in various degrees.

From the outset of his public ministry, Jesus lifted the minds of his listeners beyond the level of basal desire and cautioned them not to be distracted by inordinate concern about material things:

> So do not worry, saying, "What shall we eat?" or
> "What shall we drink?" or "What shall we wear?"
> For the Gentiles run after all these, and your heavenly
> Father knows that you need them. But seek first his

kingdom and his righteousness, and all these things will b given to you as well. Therefore do not worry about tomorrow, for tomorrow will worry about itself. Each day has enough trouble of its own. (Matthew 6:31–34)

In biblical symbolism, the heart is the eye of the body. The anxious, darting, filmy eyes of many Christians are the manifestations of a heart beclouded by the worries of this world. The translucent eyes of others radiate the simplicity and joy of a heart fixed on Jesus Christ, the Light of the world. When the author of Hebrews enjoins the reader, "Let us fix our eyes on Jesus, the author and perfecter of our faith" (Hebrews 12:2), he not only gives a simple prescription for Christian transparency but insists on a reappraisal of one's whole value system, understanding that "where your treasure is, there your heart will be also" (Luke 12:34).

Paul had the audacity to boast, "But we have the mind of Christ" (1 Corinthians 2:16). His boast was validated by his life. From the moment of Paul's conversion, Jesus Christ preoccupied his mind and heart. Christ was a force whose momentum was ceaselessly at work before Paul's eyes (Philippians 3:21). He was a person whose voice Paul could recognize (2 Corinthians 13:3); who strengthened him in his moments of weakness (2 Corinthians 12:9); who enlightened him, showed him the meaning of things, and consoled him (1 Corinthians 1:4–5). Driven to desperation by the slanderous charges of false apostles, Paul admitted to visions and revelations by the Lord Jesus (2 Corinthians 12:1). For Paul, the person of Jesus unraveled the mysteries of life and death (Colossians 3:3).

In Harper Lee's novel *To Kill a Mockingbird*, Atticus Finch says, "You'll never understand a man 'til you stand in his shoes and look at the world through his eyes." Paul looked through the eyes of Jesus Christ with such sensitivity that Christ became the ego of the apostle (Galatians 2:20).

Why should this not be so with every Christian walking in the Spirit? Paul insists that this is the normal operation of the Spirit in our lives. Transparency is the epiphany of our life in Christ Jesus; such is the sense of the beautiful imagery in Paul's second letter to the Corinthians. Amédée Brunot writes in *Saint Paul and His Message:*

> In one of the most finished passages of his correspondence, whose ease and distinction suggest the warm sunlight of Greece on the marbles of the Parthenon, Paul compares the mediation of Christ to a light whose rays shine through and transfigure his human servants (2 Corinthians 3:4ff). The radiance of Moses when he came down from Sinai was as nothing compared with the transfiguration of the Christian.

*This transfiguration became a transparency in
which faces were mingled and friendships merged.
It was a passionate embrace (Philippians 3:12–13).
From now on, the Christian's heart beats in tune with
the heart of Christ.*

Paul was a living witness to a not-uncommon phenomenon of human existence—we come to resemble those we love.

The Life of Christ

"On the last and greatest day of the Feast, Jesus stood and said in a loud voice, 'If anyone is thirsty, let him come to me and drink. Whoever believes in me, as the Scripture has said, streams of living water will flow from him'" (John 7:37–38). As long as Jesus was still trammeled by the human limitations of mortal flesh, he could not become, in the bold words of Paul, "the Son of God with power" (Romans 1:4). He could not be glorified until he had been crucified. The whole purpose of his redemptive suffering, death, and resurrection was to share with us the fruits of his Easter triumph.

In the glorification of Jesus there is what Edward Schillebeeckx has called a "handing over of power": the Father bestows his kingly might on Christ, whom he makes to be *Kyrios*. The Lord Jesus then pours out the Holy Spirit to form the holy People of God, a community of prophets and lovers who will surrender to the mystery of the fire of the Spirit that burns within, who will live in ever greater fidelity to the shattering, omnipresent Word, who will enter into the center of all that is, into the very heart and mystery of God, into the center of that flame that consumes and purifies and sets all aglow with peace, joy, boldness, and extravagant love.

"Do not put out the Spirit's fire," exhorts Paul (1 Thessalonians 5:19). To resist the Holy Spirit is to nullify the power of the paschal mystery and make sport of the greatest act of love the world has ever known. In John's Gospel, the only sin mentioned is blasphemy— the conscious, deliberate rejection of the Spirit of God.

Yet as the Franciscan Robert Powell and others have noted, the church has been updated but not renewed. The church-at-large still scans the horizon awaiting the fiery glow of the new Pentecost. The Communist who accepts Karl Marx but not his doctrine is scarcely different from the Christian who accepts Jesus Christ but refuses to shape his life according to Christ's teaching.

Paul wrote to the Philippians: "For, as I have often told you before and now say again even with tears, many live as enemies of the cross of Christ. Their destiny is destruction, their god is their stomach, and their glory is their shame. Their mind is on earthly things" (Philippians 3:18–19). Paul's cheeks are still streaked because of the tepidity, rank insincerity, spiritual adultery, indifference to prayer, ignorance of God's Word, comfortable piety, and apostolic sloth that dapple the Christian life in America today.

When Jesus Christ reveals himself through the gospel, which is active and creative, he calls for a spontaneous response. His message is not a reassurance to keep right on doing what we've been doing, but, writes Edward O'Connor, "a summons to the labor of eliminating from our lives, faithfully and perseveringly, everything in us that is opposed to the work and will of his Holy Spirit for us."

Faith means that we are ready to act on the Word. Jesus is adamant:

> Not everyone who says to me "Lord, Lord" will enter
> the Kingdom of heaven, but only he who does the will
> of my Father who is in heaven. Many will say to me
> on that day, "Lord, Lord, did we not prophecy in your
> name, and in your name drive out demons and per-
> form many miracles?" Then I will tell them plainly,
> "I never knew you. Away from me, you evildoers!"
>
> Therefore everyone who hears these words of mine
> and puts them into practice is like a wise man who
> built his house on the rock. The rain came down, the
> streams rose, and the winds blew and beat against
> that house; yet it did not fall, because it had its
> foundation on the rock. But everyone who hears these

*words of mine and does not put them into practice is
like a foolish man who built his house on sand. The
rain came down, the streams rose, and the winds blew
and beat against that house, and it fell with a great
crash. (Matthew 7:21–27)*

Authentic, evangelical faith cannot be separated
from a readiness to act on the Word of God according
to present opportunities. Whenever faith is accepted
merely as a closed system of well-defined doctrines, we
lose contact with the living God. The faith that saves is
a surrender to God. "To say 'yes' in faith implies a constant setting out," writes Bernard Haring, "an ever-
renewed readiness to receive the Word of Jesus and
act on it."

Søren Kierkegaard, the father of Christian existen-
tialism, describes two types of Christians: those who
imitate Jesus Christ and a second, much cheaper
brand—those who are content to admire him. The late
Raymond Nogar's distinction between the picture people and the drama people matches Kierkegaard's. The
picture people view the gospel safely and from a distance, as one would view Salvador Dali's *Last Supper* at
the National Gallery of Art in Washington DC. The
drama people are no mere spectators but like the audience engrossed in the Greek tragedy *Antigone* are
caught up personally in the drama of Jesus's death and
resurrection.

Often the rhetoric we use to describe our life in Christ bears only a thin resemblance to where we really are. We boast of what we are giving because it hides what we are withholding. We allow ourselves to believe that we are capable of love just because we are capable of devout sentiment. Thomas Merton writes:

> One dimension of this convenient spirituality is our total insistence on ideals and intentions, in complete divorce from reality, from actions, and from social commitment. Whatever we interiorly desire, whatever we dream, whatever we imagine: that is the beautiful, the godly and the true. Pretty thoughts are enough. They substitute for everything else including charity, including life itself.

We see avarice, rampant greed, and the exploitation of the poor on a community level. Frequently, our response is to denounce others and walk away from them, though we are all implicated.

The gospel presses us to painful honesty. If nothing else, we ought to be sincere. Get out and pant with the moneymaking street, become hedonists, and "eat, drink, and be merry for tomorrow we die," *or* repent and return to the spirit of the gospel. We are called to live as prophets and lovers in the Spirit of Jesus Christ. We can't live a lie. We are cheating the universal church and the local ecclesial community of what it expects of us. "What the gospel of Jesus Christ offers us," Thomas Merton observes, "is not a false peace which enables us to avoid the implacable light of judgment, but the grace to courageously accept the bitter truth that is revealed to us; to abandon our inertia, our egoism, and submit entirely to the demands of the Spirit, praying earnestly for help, and giving ourselves generously to every effort asked of us by God."

Paul writes to the Thessalonians: "We have passed God's scrutiny, and he has seen fit to entrust us with the work of preaching; when we speak, it is with this in view; we would earn God's good opinion, not man's, since it is God who can read our inmost thoughts" (1 Thessalonians 2:4). Here is the essence of perfect sincerity in conduct—to care for nothing but God's judgment on our actions, not to vary our attitude to suit the company we are in, not to hold one opinion when alone and adopt another in conversation, but to speak and act as in the sight of God who can read our inmost thoughts. Sincerity means trying to make the outward man more and more like the inner man by simply being true to ourselves, so that no human respect can make us false.

Early in Christian history Saint Augustine complained, "Many who had already come close on the way to believing are frightened away by the bad lives of evil and false Christians. How many, my brothers, do you think there are who want to become Christians but are put off by the evil ways of Christians?" If the searcher after truth finds Christians to be just as self-absorbed, guilt-ridden, hopeless, unsure of their foundations, and haunted by the same fears as he is, just as much at sea in an alien environment, and just as perplexed generally, it is small wonder that he feels no attraction to the church. A twenty-three-year-old woman doing graduate work at the University of Paris wrote the following:

> *To me a Christian is either a man who lives in Christ or a phony. You Christians do not appreciate that it is on this—the almost external testimony that you give of God—that we judge you. You ought to radiate Christ. Your faith ought to flow out to us like a river of life. You ought to infect us with a love for him. It is then that God who was impossible becomes possible for the atheist and for those of us whose faith is wavering. We cannot help being struck, upset, and confused by a Christian who is truly Christlike. And we do not forgive him when he fails to be.*

The woman unknowingly reiterated what Cardinal Emmanuel Suhard wrote in a 1947 pastoral: "The great mark of a Christian is what no other characteristic can replace, namely the example of a life which can only be explained in terms of God."

It is symptomatic that, despite the church having been around for two thousand years, the mass of people still pass Christianity by. Why? Because the visible presence of Jesus Christ is rarely present in Christians as a whole. We will never move people to Jesus Christ and the gospel merely by making speeches about them. Edward Schillebeeckx is blunt: "People, to put it bluntly, have had their bellyful of our sermonizing. They want a source of strength for their lives. We can only recommend this strength by making it actively present in our own lives." Contact with Christians should be an experience that proves to people that the gospel is a power that transforms the whole of life. Instead, our presence in the world is often marked by rank insincerity, a dilution of grace, and a failure to act on the Word.

The Word of God is pointed: "I hold this against you: you have forsaken your first love. Remember the height from which you have fallen! Repent and do the things you did at first" (Revelation 2:4–5). Paul expresses similar displeasure and apprehension over the faith of the Corinthians: "I am afraid that just as Eve was deceived by the serpent's cunning, your minds may somehow be led astray from your sincere and pure devotion to Christ" (2 Corinthians 11:3). Here was a man who truly acted on the Word of God. He cared only for the judgment of Jesus Christ and nothing for the judgment of men. He was more concerned about the good pleasure or displeasure of the living God than his neighbors' approval.

Paul is a courageous witness to the reality of the invisible God and a powerful example to many of us who are so influenced by the opinions of others and so interested in keeping a certain image in the community's eye, who desire only to be liked and accepted by any group with which we associate, and who are not especially careful about our image in God's sight. Otherwise, we would not so often neglect the things that God alone sees, like private prayer and secret acts of kindness. "The want of a pure intention," writes Merton, "subtly spoils everything we do, so that our life is half a lie. We can never be at ease with ourselves. But the utter sincerity of doing things that no one can ever know about just as well as the things people can see indicates a high degree of holiness."

Scripture is not about the transmission of inert ideas. It is a call to love, and love that does not lead to action is not love. Every day of our lives the Word is an imperative to rediscover the truth that, in the words of Hans Kung, "the whole secret and center of human existence remains the person of Jesus Christ."

In my own mind, the greatest need in the church today is to know Jesus Christ as Lord and Savior. This is the burden of the entire doctrine of Saint John's Gospel, "that you may believe that Jesus is the Christ, the Son of God, and that by believing you may have life in his name" (John 20:31). But this knowledge is more than a casual acknowledgment that Jesus lived and died and rose again. It is the kind of knowledge that leaves us changed. It is an encounter with someone who alters the very course of our lives. "It is not uncommon," as Ralph Martin notes, "for many Christians to have a seriously incomplete idea of what the Scriptures say about Jesus Christ. Many have a vague idea of Jesus as 'a good guy' who helped the poor and told people to love one another. They operate with a fuzzy, almost symbolic notion of Jesus as the symbol for a liberal's idea of goodness." Those who say, "Jesus would never hurt anyone," often mean to rule out the possibility that he would ever ask someone to repent or go through the pain of recognizing his brokenness. To believe that all Jesus calls us to is to be nice to each other is to substitute the Christ of Christian humanism for the Christ of Saint Paul.

In Hebrews, we read, "Let us throw off everything that hinders and the sin that so easily entangles, and let us run with perseverance the race marked out for us" (Hebrews 12:1). In the same letter, we are told, "Worship God acceptably with reverence and awe, for our 'God is a consuming fire'" (Hebrews 12:28–29). This is no Christ the humanitarian, Christ the master of interpersonal relationships, or Christ the buddy. It is Christ the Lord and Savior who calls us to repent, change our lives, and strike out in a new direction. Writes F. X. Durrwell: "This knowledge of Jesus Christ as saving Lord is the only knowledge that has any worth for us."

Continual Conversion

Most failures to act on the Word can be traced to ignorance, inattention, or insufficient esteem for the person of Christ. A loose goodwill toward the world replaces the radical conversion and explicit death to self that the gospel demands. We do not want a God who would change us or challenge us. Authentic Christianity rings in the First Letter to the Corinthians: "Jews demand miraculous signs and Greeks look for wisdom, but we preach Christ crucified: a stumbling block to Jews and foolishness to Gentiles, but to those whom God has called, both Jews and Greeks, Christ the power of God and the wisdom of God" (1 Corinthians 1:22–24). If the People of God are not hearing the call to repentance or claiming their power to fulfill it, is it because we ministers of the Word are preaching another Christ from the pulpit?

There is nobody in the Christian community who is not called to continual conversion. There is no one who does not still have before him the labor of building up the image of Jesus Christ in his life by the steady practice, day by day, of Christian virtues. And as Edward O'Connor remarks, "You don't sing your way around that stuff." Paul writes in First Corinthians, "I beat my body and make it my slave so that after I have preached to others, I myself will not be disqualified for the prize"

(1 Corinthians 9:27). To the Galatians: "Do not be deceived: God cannot be mocked. A man reaps what he sows" (Galatians 6:7).

The tone of the Christ of God is not always sweet and consoling. The gospel is the Good News of gratuitous salvation, but it does not promise a picnic on a green lawn. In the man Jesus, in his words, the invisible God becomes audible. And God convulsed the whole being of Jesus in the cry, "The kingdom of God is near. Repent and believe the good news" (Mark 1:15).

Christianity, then, comprises more than involvement in human rights struggles, environmental causes, or peace programs. Fullness of life in the Spirit is more than finding Christ in others and serving him there. It is a summons to personal holiness, ongoing conversion, and new creation through union with Christ Jesus. "Therefore, if anyone is in Christ, he is a new creation; the old has gone, the new has come" (2 Corinthians 5:17).

For this reason, the Gospel of John is especially relevant to contemporary Christians. Why? Because, in contrast with the synoptics, as John McKenzie notes, "John's Gospel is not the gospel of the Kingdom but the gospel of Jesus himself." It is impossible to exaggerate the central position of Jesus in the fourth Gospel—central not merely insofar as he is the principal protagonist and teacher, but as he illumines every page of it. In his thought-provoking book *The Art and Thought of John,*

Edgar Bruns writes, "The reader is, as it were, blinded by the brilliance of his image and comes away like a man who has looked long at the sun—unable to see anything but its light." Again, for John the only sin is to resist the Holy Spirit, reject Jesus Christ, and fail to act on his Word.

The dominant theme of the second part of John's Gospel is union with the Lord. Through the beautiful imagery of the vine and the branches, Jesus calls all people to himself. "Abide in me, dwell in me, resort to me, come to me," he beckons (see John 15:4ff). Significantly, Jesus does not say, "Come to a day of renewal, a retreat, a prayer meeting, a liturgy," but "come to *me*." Is this the self-flattering superiority of a religious fanatic? Yes, if he is not the Savior of the world. He is either an egoist or the Risen Lord who must be proclaimed as the world's only hope. No one else would dare to say:

I am the way, I am truth and life. (John 14:6)

I am the light of the world. (John 8:12)

I am the bread of heaven. He who eats of this bread will never know what it is to die. (John 6:51)

He who believes in me will have everlasting life; and the one who does not believe in me will be condemned. (John 3:35)

In captivity, Paul could think of nothing greater than to wish for the Ephesians that, "out of his glorious riches [God] may strengthen you with power through his Spirit in your inner being, so that Christ may dwell in your hearts through faith. And I pray that you, being rooted and established in love, may have power together with all the saints, to grasp how wide and long and high and deep is the love of Christ, and to know this love that surpasses knowledge—that you may be filled to the measure of all the fullness of God" (Ephesians 3:16–19).

Paul perceived that on Judgment Day our entire life will be appraised and evaluated in terms of our personal relationship with the risen Jesus of Nazareth. For this reason, he could realistically write to the Philippians, "I consider everything a loss compared to the surpassing greatness of knowing Christ Jesus my Lord, for whose sake I have lost all things. I consider them rubbish, that I may gain Christ" (Philippians 3:8).

The Apostle was like a man obsessed: his mind was aflame with one thought and his heart aglow with one desire—to know Christ Jesus, his saving Lord. (Small wonder that for the exegete François Amity the key concept of Saint Paul is *salvation*.) Upon reflection, Paul spun around and told the Colossians to wait a minute: "Since, then, you have been raised with Christ, set your hearts on things above, where Christ is seated at the right hand of God. Set your minds on things above, not on earthly things. For you died, and your life is now hidden with Christ in God. When Christ, who is your life, appears, then you also will appear with him in glory" (Colossians 3:1–4). The Christ of Paul was not merely a great teacher, an example of a great man, or a symbol of man's noblest aspirations; he was Lord and Savior. To reinterpret Jesus any other way is to bleed Christianity of its point.

3.

Diversions

There are certain burning questions that every Christian must answer in total candor. Do you hunger for Jesus Christ? Do you yearn to spend time alone with him in prayer? Is he the most important person in your life? Does he fill your soul like a song of joy? Is he on your lips as a shout of praise? Or has he been smothered by distractions, nullified by pride? Do you eagerly turn to his memoirs, his Testament, to learn more of him? Do you thirst for the living water of his Holy Spirit? Are you making the effort to die daily to anything and everything that inhibits, diminishes, or threatens your friendship with him?

To ascertain where you really are with the Lord, recall what *saddened* you the past month. Was it the realization that you do not love Jesus enough? That you did not seek his face in prayer often enough? That you did not care for his people enough? Or did you get depressed over a lack of respect, criticism from an authority figure, your finances, a lack of friends, fears about the future, or your bulging waistline?

Conversely, what *gladdened* you the past month? Reflection on your election to the Christian community? The joy of saying slowly, "Abba, Father"? The afternoon you stole away for two hours with only the gospel as your companion? A small victory over selfishness? Or were the sources of your joy a new car, a Brooks Brothers suit, a great date, great sex, a raise, or a loss of four inches from your hips?

When all Christians surrender to the mystery of the fire of the Spirit that burns within; when we submit to the saving truth that we reach life only through death, that we come to light only through darkness; when we acknowledge that the grain of wheat must fall into the ground and die, that Jonah must be buried in the whale's belly, that the alabaster jar of self must be broken if others are to perceive the sweet fragrance of Christ; when we respond to Jesus's call of "Come to me," then the limitless power of the Holy Spirit will be unleashed with astonishing force upon the church and the world.

But that will happen only when we break away from the lives we have grown accustomed to living, lives ruled by our desires for security, pleasure, and power. It is these desires that hold us back from recognizing the truth of our need for God's mercy. It is these desires that prevent us from peeling off the filmy residue of our lives without God and prevent transparency.

Security

In a very obvious sense, the security cult comprises those believers who worship more frequently at the altar of success than at the altar of the living God, who bow more regularly to the sacred cows of security and comfort than to the sovereign Lordship of Jesus Christ. The security syndrome is easily recognizable when the issue is pecuniary. One person may feel secure with only ten dollars here and now. Another person may feel insecure with $100,000 in the bank. The amount is unimportant. The kind of security we seek—whether financial, relational, career—is unimportant. What matters is the amount of time, energy, thought, and attention we invest in the unpleasant struggle to achieve the conditions we believe are indispensable for feeling secure. The details of our shopping lists are quite arbitrary. But our desire for security is very demanding and pulls our minds away from the higher calling to let our minds and hearts be inhabited by Christ Jesus.

In a less obvious sense, the hunger for security is mostly a matter of our emotional programming. My feelings of insecurity are not a necessary consequence of external circumstances (such as a business recession) or the actions of other people. The power to achieve equanimity and stability lies within me. It is not at the mercy of whim, caprice, and unpredictable external forces. What keeps me feeling insecure are my addictive emotional needs, which must always be satisfied. When reality does not live up to my expectations, I become frustrated, angry, bitter, anxious, and resentful.

For example, say you meet me on the street and tell me you found this book to be a complete waste of your time and money. Your criticism triggers my inside programming, and I sink into a swamp of sadness, self-pity, and depression. Reality has not lived up to my expectations. I anticipated at least constructive criticism, possibly appreciation, and maybe even praise. But you are not the one who has destroyed my inner equilibrium. *I did that.* Inordinately attached to my preconception of what I need to feel secure (in this case, your approval) and willfully convinced of the way the world should run, I have needlessly deprived myself of the fruits of the Holy Spirit and the abundant life that Jesus promised.

The Lord passed through the world as a figure of light and truth, sometimes tender, sometimes angry, always just, loving, and effective, but not insecure. A word, a gesture, a few syllables traced in sand, a command like "Come, follow me!" and destinies were changed, spirits reborn. He chatted with Samaritans, prostitutes, and children and spoke to them of truth and mercy and forgiveness with never a shadow of insecurity darkening his countenance. Spending time with those who attracted the disapproval of all, he never wavered from his desire to offer them his kingdom.

When we cling to a miserable sense of security, the possibility of transparency is utterly defeated. Just as the sunrise of faith requires the sunset of our former unbelief, our false ideas, and our erroneous and circumscribed convictions, so the dawn of trust requires the abandonment of our craving for material and spiritual reassurances. Security in the Lord Jesus implies that we no longer calculate or count the cost.

The kind of trust that depends on the response it receives is a bogus trust, one based only in anxiety. In trembling insecurity, the believer pleads for and even demands tangible reassurances from the Lord that his affection is returned. If he does not receive them, he is disheartened, frustrated, maybe even convinced that it's all over or that it never really existed. If he does receive them, he is reassured, but only for a time. He presses for further proofs—each one less convincing than the one that went before. In the end this false trust dies of pure frustration.

What the insecure Christian has not learned is that tangible reassurances, however valuable they may be, cannot create trust, sustain it, or provide any certainty of its presence. Jesus Christ calls us to hand over our autonomous selves in complete confidence. Only when that decision is ratified and the craving for reassurances is stifled are transparency, certainty, and peace achieved.

The mystery of the Lord's Ascension contains an important lesson for the security-obsessed. Jesus said to his disciples, "I tell you the sober truth: it is much better for you that I go" (John 16:7). Why? How could Jesus's departure profit the apostles? Primarily because if he failed to go, "the Counselor will not come to you; but if I go, I will send him to you" (John 16:7). Secondarily because while he was still visible on earth, there was always the danger that the apostles would become so wedded to the sight of his human flesh that they would leave the certainty of faith and lean on the tangible evidence of the senses. To see Jesus in the flesh was good, but "more blessed are they who have not seen and have believed" (John 20:29).

In the winter of 1952, during some of the heaviest combat of the Korean War, two Marine corporals were crouched in the bunker of a forward observation post some one hundred yards inside enemy lines. Jack

Robison and Tim Casey had been friends for almost a year. They met in ammunition-demolition school in Quantico, Virginia, went on furlough together, then traveled on to Camp Pendleton, California, for advanced infantry training. Their regiment had arrived in Pusan in the fall of 1951.

It was a little after midnight, and a light snow was falling. Huddled in the bunker, the two were passing a cigarette back and forth when a hand grenade, lobbed by an undetected North Korean twenty-five yards north of their position, landed squarely between them. Casey spotted it first. He nonchalantly flicked the butt aside and fell on the grenade. It detonated instantly, but Casey's stomach absorbed the explosion. He winked at Robison and rolled over dead.

Four years later Robison entered religious life. When he pronounced his solemn vows in 1960, he took a new name to symbolize his new life in Christ Jesus. He changed his given name from Jack to Casey in the hope that the spirit of self-sacrifice that had animated Tim Casey's life would characterize his own. He also befriended Casey's widowed mother and began to divide his Christmas vacations between his own family in Rhode Island and Mrs. Casey in Chicago.

One summer Father Casey Robison dropped in at Mrs. Casey's on a surprise visit. He was feeling tired and depressed. They followed the usual procedure of watching the afternoon soap operas on television together, holding hands all the while. After dinner they sat in the living room having a drink and reminiscing about the days when Tim was alive. The priest's depression lingered. Unexpectedly he asked, "Ma, do you think Casey really loved me?"

She laughed. "Oh, Jack, ya sure got a way with ya." It was a faint Irish brogue. "Ya can't ever be serious."

"I am serious," Robison replied.

There was fear in her eyes. "Now stop funnin' me, Jack."

"I'm not funnin', Ma."

She looked at him in disbelief. Then fear turned to fury. Mrs. Casey never cussed or took the Lord's name casually. But that night she stood up and screamed, "Jesus Christ, man, what more could he ha' done fer ya?"

Then she sank back in the chair, buried her head in her bosom, and began to sob. Over and over again the same phrase was endlessly, unbearably repeated: "What more could he ha' done fer ya?"

After what seemed a long time, she smiled her wan little smile and said softly, "Ah, Jack, I guess we all need those reassurances from time to time."

That was the night Father Casey Robison gave up his insecurity and found the peace that comes with genuine trust.

"The devil never rejoices more," said Francis of Assisi, "than when he robs a servant of God of his peace of heart." Peace and joy go a-begging when the heart of a Christian longs for one sign after another of God's merciful love. Nothing is taken for granted and nothing is received with gratitude. The troubled eyes and furrowed brow of the anxious believer are the symptoms of a heart where trust has not found a home. The Lord himself must pass through all the shades of the emotional spectrum with us, from rage to tears to amusement. But the poignant truth remains—we do not trust him. We do not have the mind of Christ Jesus. "Do not be afraid, little flock, for your Father has been pleased to give you the kingdom" (Luke 12:32).

The words of Mrs. Casey ought to be enough for us as well: "Jesus Christ, what more could he ha' done fer ya?"

Insecurity not only paralyzes our relationship with the living God but has a devastating effect on interpersonal relationships. It is the starting point of all social estrangement. It breaks down openness, which is the bridge to the existential world of the other. It undermines real communication and causes a kind of rupture in the evolution of authentic personality. Ken Keyes Jr. writes:

> The security center is such a lonely level of consciousness. When your consciousness is preoccupied with striving toward what you feel to be your security needs, you are more isolated from people than at any other level. And your energy will be at its

lowest. When you are preoccupied with security, you are trapped in conflicting conditions in your relationships with others. You create "others" as objects to help you become more secure—or as objects to fight because they threaten your security. On the security level you cannot love others since this level creates great distances between you and other people.

The insecure Christian finds it exceedingly difficult to listen to the opinions of others. He is so uncertain about his own identity that he has to assert himself all the time, gripped as he is by the fear that in listening to others or surrendering an opinion he may lose a part of his own shaky identity. Or his uncertainty about his identity may cause him to rarely assert himself, since expressing his true feelings to others might open him up to their criticism. He seldom laughs at himself because hearty laughter (the built-in safety valve reminding him of his creaturehood) is a luxury he cannot indulge: it might reduce his overestimation of himself and impel him to stop taking himself so seriously. He does not cry—that would be a chink in his "invulnerable" armor. Conversely, he may cry often, but alone—he can't let others know that he is less than perfect. He does not readily admit mistakes because of his insatiable desire for the approval of others. Blunders damage his credibility. "We live in an age," says J. B. Priestley, "when no man of importance ever admits that he is wrong."

Why are so many Christians mummified by middle age? Why do we stop growing in the spiritual dimension of our lives? Why do our liturgies become so stagnant and our prayer meetings so stylized? Why have creativity and flexibility given way to repetition and rigidity? Where is the life lived as new creations?

We trot out once more what worked in the past. The breath of God is bottled and the gallivanting Spirit is stymied. The new, the creative, the fresh is looked on with suspicion, not with fascination. "To live is to change," wrote John Henry Newman, "and to have lived well is to have changed often." But the fear of failure prevents any surprise by the Spirit. The Nobel Prize–winning physicist Max Planck said that the long labyrinthine path that led to the discovery of the quantum theory would never have been traversed if his research team had been afraid of making mistakes. In the lives of many Christians, apprehension about making mistakes stunts growth, stifles the Spirit, and ensures the progressive narrowing of their personalities.

The church of Jesus Christ is a place of promise and possibility, of adventure and discovery, a community of love on the move, strangers and exiles in a foreign land en route to the heavenly Jerusalem. But the security seekers are the enemies of openness. Their insistence on preserving the status quo thwarts innovation and spontaneity and discourages the exploration of new roads into the mind of Christ Jesus; wanting to keep things the way they are automatically introduces a new insecurity with more cautions, threats, and nervous tension.

Saint John calls this addiction to security "darkness" because it sets itself in opposition to the Light. He pleads "that they may all be one, Father, just as you are in me and I am in you. May they also be in us so that the world may believe that you have sent me" (John 17:21). Living dependent on "security" defeats carefree trust in God's wisdom and love, hurts interpersonal relationships, thwarts ongoing community renewal and Christian reunion, and handicaps the serious Christian who seeks to have the mind of Christ Jesus.

Pleasure

Once we have shuttered all the windows, bolted the doors, and tightened the nuts and bolts on our mental machinery, we begin to feel secure. But eventually the ennui and quiet desperation of our hermetically sealed existence drive us to seek compensation and satisfaction through all kinds of pleasurable experiences. When forms of pleasure, leisure, and recreation refresh mind and body and revitalize the spirit, they bring a sense of balance, rest, and wholeness. But sought after for themselves, they send us on a roller-coaster ride during which each sensation must be greater than the last one for the thrill to continue.

Sex may be the most sought after pleasure, followed by the mellowing effect of alcohol or the energy boost of drugs. For some, pleasure is found in the comfort of food. For others, it is life lived through music or movies that give us access to our deeply buried emotional lives.

How easily this quest for pleasure turns into obsession and obsession into a kind of soul death:

> *Those who live according to the sinful nature have their minds set on what that nature desires; but those who live in accordance with the Spirit have their minds set on what the Spirit desires. The mind of sinful man is death, but the mind controlled by the Spirit is life and peace; the sinful mind is hostile to God. It does not submit to God's law, nor can it do so. Those controlled by the sinful nature cannot please God. (Romans 8:5–8)*

The carnal man is blatantly in the flesh and lives and walks according to the flesh. Yet many Christians practice an ambivalent "prudence of the flesh" that seeks a sort of gilded mediocrity: the self is carefully distributed between flesh and spirit, with a watchful eye on both. Paul calls this "imperfect spiritual vision." It is the vision of those who have received the Spirit but remain spiritual infants because they do not subject themselves fully to the domination of the Spirit; they yield to their passions, thus letting their drives confine them to an infantile spirituality. Paul compares them to babies unable to take solid food (1 Corinthians 3:2). "The perfect Christian," writes Jean Mouroux, "is he who does not normally yield to the demands of the flesh, and who is normally docile to the impulses of the Spirit."

One of the more intriguing forms of self-indulgence is narcissistic obsession with our bodies. Proceeding from a valid and important interest in maintaining our health, we nevertheless spend a staggering amount of time and energy on acquiring or maintaining a fit figure. Napoleon's mapping strategy for the invasion of Russia was an amateur tactical effort compared to the ingenuity, skill, and logistic precision of the body-conscious. No sudden snack is unforeseen, no workout unplanned, no carb or calorie unaccounted for. Professional guidance is procured, books and periodicals scrutinized, health clubs subsidized, plastic surgery pondered, and the merits of the fashionable diet of the day debated on national television. What is a rich spiritual life compared to the exquisite sensation of looking like a celebrity? To paraphrase Cardinal Wolsey, "Would that I had served my God the way I have watched my waistline."

Of course, preoccupation with one's physical appearance bears no resemblance to the mind of Jesus Christ.

The Lord experiences only sadness and compassion for our pathetic pursuit of physical sensation. And our efforts to find excitement and ignite passion don't end with the physical. We Christians are as prone to chemical dependency, affairs, self-serving friendships, and risky behavior as those who don't claim to hold Christ in their hearts. We seek and search for ways to fill up the gaping holes in our lives, yet come away from these experiences with little more than a temporary sense of completion.

The absence of a divine love experience is painfully apparent. Whether we seek to fill the void with blatantly fleshly pursuits, such as illicit sex, alcohol, or drugs, or fool ourselves into believing our drive for pleasure is based in spiritual preference, the name of the game is the same.

Consider how our churches have explored and exploited our need to replace the numbness in our lives with a passion for something, anything. We've created worship in which the music is meant to stir the emotions but the soul is left unmoved, in which the words spoken are little more than manipulations of the heart. We have created cathartic experiences filled with weeping and dancing in the Spirit that leave us with the sense that we have touched God but that fail to give us the sense that God has touched us. We run to churches where the message feels good and where we feel energized and uplifted—but never challenged or convicted. "It is not surprising that spiritual experiences are mushrooming all over the place and have become highly sought-after commercial items," writes Henri Nouwen. "Many people flock to places and persons who promise intensive experiences of togetherness, cathartic emotions of exhilaration and sweetness, and liberating sensations of rapture and ecstasy. In our desperate need for fulfillment and our restless search for the experience of divine intimacy, we are all too prone to construct our own spiritual events."

Power

The last desire that hinders us from putting on the mind of Jesus Christ is the lust for power. In his ministry, Jesus rejected any display of power except the power of the Holy Spirit. Unlike "the kings of the Gentiles [who] lord it over them" (Luke 22:25), the disciples were not to exercise authority. The Lord himself performed the menial service of the slave at the door by washing the dusty feet of his disciples, then required them to do the same. "Now that I, your Lord and Teacher, have washed your feet, you also should wash one another's feet. I have set you an example that you should do as I have done for you" (John 13:14–15).

When Jesus appropriated to himself the "Ebed Yahweh" title of Isaiah (see Luke 22:24–30), he strengthened the servant identification by leading a little child into the group and telling the disciples they must learn to resemble him. John McKenzie notes:

> *The sharpness of this answer has not always been appreciated. Effectively Jesus says there is no "first" in the Reign of God. If you want to be first, become every man's lackey; return to your childhood, and then you will be fit for the first place. Jesus leaves little room for ambition; and he leaves no more room for the exercise of power. Lackeys and children are not bearers of power.*

The power games we play, whether gross or subtle, are directed toward dominating people and situations, thereby increasing our prestige, influence, and reputation. Our myriad methods of manipulation, control, and passive aggression create a life that is little more than a series of competitive moves and countermoves. We have convinced ourselves that we must have power in order to be happy. We have developed a fine radar system attuned to the actions and vibrations of any person or situation that even remotely threatens our position of authority. Our ineffectiveness in developing deeply loving relationships—with others as well as with God—is rooted in our power addiction. We perceive other people as objects that either enhance or endanger our prestige, as pawns to be advanced or eliminated according to whether they protect their leader and hasten or hinder the victorious sweep across the board of life. What a friend of mine calls "the king-baby syndrome"—the emotional programming that seeks to compensate for the power deficiency we experienced as children—leads to a preoccupation with status symbols like expensive cars, the latest tech gadgets, and custom-built houses. It motivates us to accumulate money as a method of wielding power.

Yet the quest for power is not limited to material gains or the drive to rule a personal empire. The pull of power is the force behind the desire to acquire knowledge as a means of achieving recognition as an "interesting" person. Knowledge can be power even in the spiritual life. The expert knows that she must be consulted before any definitive judgment can be made. The game of one-upmanship prevents the interchange of ideas and introduces a spirit of rivalry and competition that is all too human. But power games come at the cost of deep connection with our brothers and sisters. We cannot journey with those we disdain without someone being left in the dust.

A recent psychological portrait of successful American entrepreneurs revealed four common characteristics: (1) they are largely displaced persons—immigrants or exiles from their native countries; (2) they possess an inner locus of control that impels them to play an active part in shaping their own destiny; (3) they are encouraged by the example of less-talented businesspeople who have carved out new careers; and (4) they have adequate resources. The same eminently human qualities may stamp Christians who seek authority and power within the spiritual community. As exiles in a foreign land who cannot own our secular culture and are driven by the need to dominate others in order to be happy, goaded by the Cinderella success of less-gifted brothers and sisters who have risen to leadership roles, and resourceful in political and clerical intrigue, we feign acquiescence to the will of God.

These power ploys are predictable. We boast of our alleged achievements while disclaiming any personal credit, vaunt our gifts of discernment and beseech prayers for continued enlightenment, manifest extraordinary pseudo-serenity in the face of adversity, and meekly protest the burdens of leadership.

The will to power is subtle. It may go unrecognized and undetected and therefore unchallenged. But Christians who succeed in seizing power, collecting disciples, acquiring knowledge, achieving status and prestige, and controlling the world are estranged from the mind of Jesus. We grow fearful when a disciple swipes our baton, cynical when feedback is negative, paranoid when threatened, fitful when challenged, and distraught when defeated. Though we live fully in the flesh ourselves, we discount criticism as not being "in the Spirit." Christians who are successful in the power game live a hollow life: there is considerable evidence of external success on the outside, but the inside is desolate, unloving, and anxiety-ridden. King-baby seeks to master God rather than be mastered by God. The tragedy lies in our flagrant attempts to contradict the Lord.

Wilfred Owen, a twenty-five-year-old British officer who died in battle just before the 1918 armistice, masterfully described in "The Parable of the Old Man and the Young" the desire for power by reconstructing the Genesis narrative of the sacrifice of Isaac:

> *So Abram rose, and clave the wood, and went,*
> *And took the fire with him, and a knife.*
> *And as they sojourned both of them together,*
> *Isaac the first-born spake and said, My Father,*
> *Behold the preparations, fire and iron,*
> *But where is the lamb for this burnt-offering?*
> *Then Abram bound the youth with belts and straps,*
> *And builded parapets and trenches there,*
> *And stretched forth the knife to slay his son.*
> *When lo! an angel called him out of heaven,*
> *Saying, Lay not thy hand upon the lad,*
> *Neither do anything to him, Behold,*
> *A ram, caught in a thicket by its horns;*
> *Offer the Ram of Pride instead of him.*
>
> *But the old man would not do so, but slew his son,*
> *And half the seed of Europe, one by one.*

"The old man would not do so!" we protest. And still we persist in our efforts to contradict God, crazily choosing death over life, stasis over dynamism, domination over submission, power over surrender. But God refuses to let us have the last word in anything. And that is God's prerogative. We think we can utter the last word, so God contradicts whatever "absolute word" we speak, whatever "ultimate thing" we do. The biblical narrative shows this clearly: God contradicts our death thrust, holds back our arm, opens up a new door, shows us a new path. That is why the power seeker is doomed to frustration.

"Those seeking to respond to the Spirit's call for renewal and restoration must be ever so careful that self-seeking, resentment, frustration, and desire for power do not lead them beyond what is truly from the Spirit of God," Ralph Martin writes. "The tragic example of renewal movements throughout church history that developed a spirit of pride and rebellion and so brought curse as well as blessing to the Christian people must be ever before us."

Life driven by our desire for security, pleasure, and power dims the Light within us and introduces unnecessary mental and emotional sufferings, which are often misconstrued as spiritual trials or the inevitable growth pains of life in the Spirit. This is erroneous discernment. They are born of our own will, not the will of God. The anxious striving for security, the vehement pursuit of physical and spiritual pleasure, and the desperate bid for power banish peace and joy, serenity and self-possession, gentleness, patience, and the other fruits of the Holy Spirit. The gospel of Jesus Christ promises no relief, deliverance, or fulfillment for these self-inflicted maladies apart from full submission to the mind of Christ. They must be surgically uprooted in their very center, and the power to perform the operation is ours. It is not the stuff of circumstances that steals our Promethean fire but our incessant addictions, needs, and desires.

In his book *Inner Healing*, Michael Scanlan says:

> *Frequently, people have others pray for them, asking for tranquility, calmness, stability, understanding, tolerance, joy, freedom from anxiety, resentments, or guilt but nothing appears to happen. People are naturally inclined to seek after such desirable goods the way they would academic degrees, business success, or physical development with the additional point that they seek through God rather than through other [people]. This is not the way to inner healing by the Lord. The Lord has his gift for us and we must adjust to accepting his gift. We don't determine what we want and how we will attain it. We decide to accept the Lord's gift and do whatever is necessary so that we will receive and retain it.*

The journey to transparency requires that we humbly acknowledge, before God, that we are inordinately preoccupied with security, pleasure, and power. It requires genuine compassion for others when we see them acting out their addictions and emotion-backed demands; it is our inner solidarity in darkness that reduces self-righteousness and irritability and makes compassion possible. The journey to transparency begins with an honest confrontation with the truth, which is not *something* we acquire, but *Someone*.

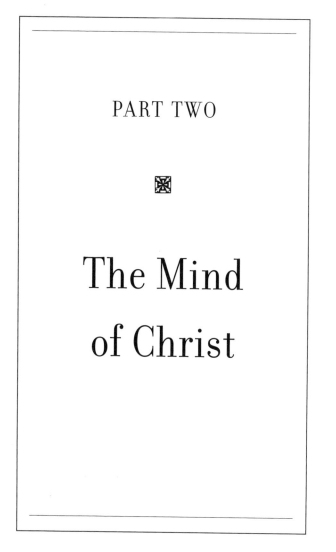

PART TWO

The Mind
of Christ

4.

Finding
the Father

Learning to think like Jesus is, naturally, no small thing. Yet we often live as though we have a firm grasp of something so utterly outside of our own way of understanding and acting. As if such a thing were possible! So let us move ahead with the assumption that we search the mind of Christ knowing that full understanding is an impossible goal. Still, there is much to discover by turning our hearts from the desires that have no place in Christ's gospel—security, plea-sure, and power—and facing instead those passions that did occupy the soul and mind of Jesus.

Jesus is not opaque about where his mind was focused:

On one occasion an expert in the law stood up to test Jesus. "Teacher," he asked, "what must I do to inherit eternal life?" "What is written in the law?" he replied. "How do you read it?" He answered: "Love the Lord your God, with all your heart and with all your soul and with all your strength and with all your mind"; and "Love your neighbor as yourself." "You have answered correctly," Jesus replied. "Do this and you will live." But he wanted to justify himself, so he asked Jesus, "And who is my neighbor?" (Luke 10:25–29)

Jesus replied with the parable of the Good Samaritan to explain the second part of the great commandment. But no one asked him to explain the *first* part of the great commandment. Even today we spend a great deal of time in our churches talking about loving our neighbors (although we spend far too little time actually doing so), and yet we rarely consider what it means to love God with all our heart, soul, strength, and mind. Perhaps the following parable can help us enter into a deeper understanding of what that kind of love might look like.

The Parable of the Medicine Man

Many years ago, in the little Mexican town of Hopi, a baby was born. The townspeople had awaited his nativity with much interest since his great-grandfather was Irish and his great-grandmother black, his grandfather was Mexican and his grandmother Creole, his father was half-Indian and his mother Spanish. The little baby had a very mixed ancestry and consequently a very funny color—a mix of white and gold, caramel and coffee. Not knowing what to call him, his parents finally named him Willie. Shortly after birth, he suffered from polio and was left partially paralyzed.

Willie learned early that children can be very cruel when they don't understand. At school they laughed at his crazy color, tweaked his burnt-orange hair, and sometimes kicked his gimpy leg. When the children played tug-of-war at the fiesta for the Virgin of the Assumption, his teammates suddenly let go so that only Willie was dragged through the slimy pool of mud. Later, in the wheelbarrow race, his partner dumped Willie into a pile of brambles with very sharp thorns.

That night Willie's mother bathed him after she had picked out all the thorns and rubbed his aching body with soothing aloe oil. As he fell asleep she caressed him tenderly and told him once again, as she had so many times before, about the great El Shaddai and his love for little children, how they flocked to him and never wanted to leave him.

As the great day of the Virgin of Guadalupe's fiesta drew near, Willie worked hard to save money from his job feeding Macho, the town donkey. On the night of the fiesta, he limped eagerly into the village square, where everyone had gathered for the celebration. His eyes danced when he saw the cotton-candy stands, the pretty ladies in their swirling hoop skirts, the prancing horses of the merry-go-round, the men's sequined sombreros worn but once a year, the colorful clown in the zebra suit dancing like a gazelle.

Willie was wandering about, debating whether to spend his meager savings on a tortilla or a tamale, when his eye caught sight of an old wooden wagon. An overhanging sign read THE GREAT MEDICINE SHOW. As Willie cautiously approached, suddenly his heart rose in his throat. A tall, gaunt, angular man stepped up on the buckboard, extended his arms, and was about to speak. Just then he looked straight at Willie. His face was weather-beaten, but his eyes! They were sad, but so piercing and gentle and kind. Willie's heart told him at once who this man was. "It is El Shaddai," cried Willie. The Medicine Man smiled. His face glowed like a sunburst, and his eyes danced merrily.

"Here, little brother," said the Medicine Man. He handed Willie a bottle filled with bright orange liquid. "Rub three drops on your heart each night, and wonderful things will happen to you." Willie reached into his pocket, prepared to offer all that he had for this bottle, but the Medicine Man said, "What I have freely received I must freely give."

The Medicine Man sat down on the buckboard. Willie approached him and asked timidly, "Will the stuff in the bottle make my crooked leg straight, señor, and make my blotches go away?"

The Medicine Man picked him up and sat him on his knee. Willie was scared now. He was afraid that when the Medicine Man saw his skin up close he would laugh, like all the villagers, who had nicknamed him Speckled Trout.

Willie was not at all prepared for what happened next. The Medicine Man drew the boy's head against his own heart. It was so warm and peaceful there that Willie thought of the fireplace in the living room of the little house where he lived. Then he felt drops of rain on his head and looked up to see tears of compassion streaming from the Medicine Man's eyes. Willie thought at once of his mother. But even with her, he had never been loved like this before.

"Little brother, what is your name?"

"Willie." The boy's head never moved from the Medicine Man's heart, and he still clutched the bottle in his hand.

"My medicine is so powerful, Willie, that not only will it straighten your leg, but it will straighten all winding paths and all crooked hearts. Every valley of pain shall be filled and every mountain of pride leveled, and all mankind shall see the salvation of God."

He touched Willie's burnt-orange hair and kissed him lightly on the forehead. "Would you like to share my dinner with me, Willie?" In his whole life, no one had ever invited Willie to dinner; in fact, no one except his mother and father had ever asked him to share anything. Feelings that Willie had never known existed welled up in his heart. Everybody else had driven him deeper and deeper into his isolation. But the Medicine Man wanted to share his meal with him. Willie was beside himself with joy. He pulled all the money out of his pocket. "I'll buy dessert," he fairly shouted. "Lemon ices, cotton candy, and dandelion cookies!"

They ate heartily. Willie talked excitedly, and the Medicine Man listened quietly. Willie spoke of his father and mother, how hard school was, how he wished he had a friend. Then he looked hard into the sad, gentle eyes and grew bold enough to ask, "Would you be my friend, señor?"

"I am your friend," answered the Medicine Man.

Without warning, a cold chill gripped Willie's heart. He had never had a friend. What if he didn't know how to be a friend? The Medicine Man was so generous and good, so kind and loving. *Surely I will fail him, and then I will lose my only friend,* thought Willie.

"Oh, señor," he said through his fear, "please tell me what it means to be a friend! I want so much to learn."

"Do not let your heart be troubled, little brother. I will tell you the kind of friend I am, and then you can decide for yourself what kind you would like to be. Willie, if I speak to you with beautiful words that make you feel important, but do not love you, I am not your friend. If I share all my knowledge with you so that you understand all the mysteries of the universe, but do not love you, I am no friend at all. If I give all my food to feed your family and take care of all your needs, but do not love you, I am not your friend.

"Little brother, I will always be patient with you. I will always be kind to you. I will never be jealous of your other friends. Even though I am the only son of my father, I will never put on airs with you. I will never be snobbish. I will never be rude to you. I will not befriend you to get what I can; I will not easily be moved to anger with you. I will not brood when you disappoint me. I will not rejoice when you do wrong things, but I will rejoice when you are true to yourself. There is no limit to my forgiveness of your faults, to my trust in you, to my hope in you, to my power to endure all the trials of friendship with you.

"Willie, listen closely now. I will never fail you. Prophecies will cease, tongues will fall silent, knowledge will pass away, but I will not forget you. I will never cease being your friend. Little brother, perhaps your memory is not so good. If you forget everything, do not forget this. There are three things that last in friendship—faith, hope, and love. And the greatest of these is love."

Willie listened attentively. "That is so beautiful, señor," he said, shaking his head. "But I'm afraid I could never be a friend like that. I am too weak, too ugly, too moody, too dumb."

"That's why I gave you my special elixir, little brother. Be sure to rub the three drops on your heart each night. The first drop is called forgiveness, the second is acceptance, and the third is joy. Do that and know that you are blessed." Then he smiled his warmest smile and departed.

Willie ran, skipped, jumped, and danced all the way home. When he arrived, he went to his room, closed the door, and knelt down beside his bed. He opened the bottle and began to rub the first drop—forgiveness of others—on his heart. It was very painful because the other children had hurt him deeply.

But soon a wondrous thing happened: Willie had been so open to the Medicine Man's friendship that the drops of orange liquid didn't rest *on* his heart, they actually entered *into* his heart. What normally took years for the Spirit of the Medicine Man to accomplish in the ordinary heart took place in Willie's open, child-like, transparent heart in an instant. All anxiety about his leg, his blotches, everything, vanished. And Willie began to pray aloud:

"Oh, señor, El Shaddai, my friend, do not leave me. You may ask anything of me. All I want is you. Just walk close beside me with your hand in my hand for friendship's sake and for the joy of being together. Even if you were teasing me about healing my leg and my blotches, I don't care. I'll be so happy to be a speckled trout if only you will stay with me. I remember the one thing you said that mattered most ... I love you, my friend. Do anything you want, señor. Only don't ever leave me. And don't ever let me leave you."

You see, after the Spirit of the Medicine Man had entered Willie's heart, it coursed through his whole being and opened his eyes to realize how empty life would be without his friend. That thought so staggered his mind and appalled his heart that Willie would never again be the same. But it also opened his eyes to see that in the depths of his heart he really had but one burning desire—not for the things that the Medicine Man had promised, but for the Medicine Man himself.

Loving God Wholeheartedly

It isn't difficult to see where this parable takes us. In Matthew's Gospel (22:34–40), when Jesus is asked to name the greatest commandment, he begins with the

Shema Israel, the words of Deuteronomy 6:5, and adds to this Leviticus 19:18, the precept of the love of neighbor. Though Jesus distinguishes these two commandments, it is obviously only for the purpose of showing how they coalesce in one and are inseparable one from the other.

If these words are interpreted as constituting a personal statement of Jesus's attitude toward his Creator and Father and the people he came to save, then Jesus embodies the great commandment. "All I want is you, señor" echoes Jesus's limitless love and unwavering obedience to God. His statement "The world must learn that I love the Father and that I do exactly what my Father has commanded me" (John 14:31) offers luminous insight into the thoughts that inhabited the mind of Christ Jesus: God is, and that is sufficient.

Living in this place of supreme rest is neither a dreamy abstraction nor an excuse for removing ourselves from the urgent needs of this world. The apostle Paul is a stark realist. He is not advising his listeners to take on a simplistic, ethereal faith when he writes, "Your attitude should be the same as that of Christ Jesus" (Philippians 2:5). Rather, this is a place of centering. In quiet listening, Christians start from where we are, discover what we have, and realize that we have already arrived. There is no need to pursue God, to beg for God to become known to us. Paul writes, "Don't you know that you yourselves are God's temple and that God's Spirit lives in you?" (1 Corinthians 3:16).

To live here is to realize that we have what we seek. There is no need to run after security, pleasure, and power, as the unbelievers do. The kingdom of God is within us. All that is necessary is to slow down to a human tempo and take time to listen. God has been there all the time.

And so we cry out with Willie, "All I want is you, señor," and with Saint Paul, "I want to know Christ" (Philippians 3:10). We pray with the Psalmist:

One thing I ask of the Lord, this is what I seek:
that I may dwell in the house of the Lord all the days
*   of my life,*
to gaze upon the beauty of the Lord
and to seek him in his temple. (Psalms 27:4)

Christians who move toward this place will find peace and pleasure in the divine Enough. Here we stop worrying about what we don't have because we are taking the time to appreciate and enjoy what we do have. The greater percentage of the unnecessary, self-induced suffering in our lives is eliminated because the addictions that once pushed us toward achieving security, experiencing pleasure, and developing power no longer assert themselves with their absurd demands for instant satisfaction. Worry and anxiety no longer drive us, for we realize they are not borne of the gospel and carry no redemptive significance. They only prolong the times of darkness in our life and can be eliminated by submitting our thoughts to the Lordship of Jesus Christ.

Of course, in our human condition we aren't always able to put our minds and hearts on the path of Christ. But we know that these ripples on the surface of our souls cannot become tidal waves when we descend into the inner sanctum of our graced selves and enter into the prayer of listening to our God, who reminds us, "Quiet your heart and be still. I am with you. Do not be afraid. I hold you in the palm of my hand. All is well."

The effect of this listening is not just internal and personal. When the outside conditions of life no longer make for security or insecurity, when the trivial and inevitable problems of the daily routine have lost their power to splinter our concentration and fragment our existence, we perceive the world as a friendlier place. We experience everyone and everything around us in a different way—not in terms of how they meet our addictive needs but as singular manifestations of truth, goodness, and beauty in the world. We live in rhythm with the mind of Christ Jesus and enter into the flow and harmony of God's creative design. George Maloney notes: "There is a great experience of unity in finding God in all things. The dichotomy between action and contemplation does not exist anymore."

The perception of God being enough is the hall-mark of the transparent life. Gone are the tensions, hassles, and struggles that signal entrapment by our basest desires. The restless scanning of the horizon for new experiences ceases; the constant churning of the mind for escapes and distractions disappears. Even the occasional lapses into egotistic thoughts are seen as opportunities for growth into a deeper connection with God. Whether acting or being acted upon, we respond with the mind of Jesus Christ. In this lies transparency.

In loving God with his whole heart, soul, mind, and strength, Jesus was utterly transparent and therefore revealed God. In Jesus there was no self to be seen, only the ultimate, unconditional love of God. The late Paul Tillich made this the criterion of the Christian claim that Jesus is the final revelation of God: "He became completely transparent to the mystery he reveals."

Our ability to put on the mind of Christ Jesus comes by virtue of our sacred union with him. This is the gift of the Holy Spirit: "God has poured out his love into our hearts by the Holy Spirit, whom he has given us" (Romans 5:5). The power to love God wholeheartedly is the birthright of those reborn in the Spirit of Jesus Christ. It is what allows us to move out into the world as crystalline bearers of God's image.

5·

A Heart of Forgiveness

One of my most vivid memories from my time with the Little Brothers of Jesus is from New Year's Day 1969. We retired early but rolled out of the sack at midnight for an hour of nocturnal adoration. The time passed quickly in songs of thanksgiving for the undeserved gift of Jesus Christ and the Holy Spirit, in reparation for the intemperance and debauchery that traditionally characterize New Year's Eve, and in earnest intercession for some friends who were living without hope.

We then gathered in the kitchen. The table was laden with fruit bread, strawberry preserves, canned peaches, and bottles of white wine. The Little Brothers of Jesus play as they pray, and it was a rollicking hour of feasting, self-deprecating humor, and camaraderie. I went to bed around two and fell asleep thinking of something the writer Paul Gallico once said—that he would readily have signed the Franciscan contract and followed the primitive rule in all its rigor, except for the impossible clause. At the end of it all Saint Francis would deny him the only satisfaction he really wanted: a haughty disdain and lusty contempt for the mediocre Christian.

New Year's morning brought the first heavy snowfall. The Saint-Remy landscape was bleak and barren. As Ernest Hemingway introduced the death motif in *Farewell to Arms* with his opening sentence "The leaves fell early that year," so nature lay dying, and 1969 seemed a very good year to die to all the values, attitudes, and behavior patterns that were not of Christ Jesus.

There were seven of us seated at the table. The conversation centered mainly on our work in the town of Montbard. Some labored in the local vineyards, others at carpentry and masonry, while the less gifted went to more prosaic employments. I washed dishes as the Hotel de la Gare and shoveled manure on a nearby farm.

The table talk grew animated when the German brother remarked that our wages were substandard and the Spaniard added that the hours were lousy. I noted that our employers were never seen in the parish church, and a French brother suggested that they were hypocritical. The salvos got heavier and the tone more caustic. We concluded that our self-sufficient patrons slept all day Sunday, spent their money without thought, and never lifted their minds and hearts in prayer to thank God for the gifts of life, faith, family, harvest, and so on.

Brother Dominique Voillaume sat at the end of the table and never opened his mouth. I saw tears rolling down his cheeks.

"What's the matter, Dominique?" we asked.

His voice was barely audible. "Ils ne comprennent pas," was all he said.

They don't understand. How many times in recent years that sentence has turned my resentment into compassion. How I have come to appreciate Paul Gallico's insight and to marvel at his honesty. How often I have reread the Passion narrative through the eyes of Dominique Voillaume and gained a new understanding of the mind of Christ Jesus. In the throes of his death agony, beaten and bullied, scourged and spat upon, surrounded by a crowd of brutes, Jesus says, "Forgive them, Father. *Ils ne comprennent pas!*" The Teacher whose attitude toward sin was so inexorable, the rigid moralist who surrounded marriage with the lofty bulwark of indissolubility, the austere judge who condemned the mere intention to do evil, the sacred man whom no breath of suspicion ever touched was not only called to be but actually was "the friend of publicans and sinners."

Judas Iscariot enters the garden with the crowd to identify the Son of Man by an embrace. Jesus appeals to his heart and then to his conscience. "Judas, would you betray the Son of Man with a kiss?" (Luke 22:48). He will not censure Judas before others. There will be no public humiliation for the treason. "Friend, do what you are here for!" is all he says.

Compassion for others and joy over their repentance reign in the mind of Christ. Jesus ended the parable of the Good Samaritan with a question: "'Which of these three do you think was a neighbor to the man who fell into the hands of the robbers?' The expert in the law replied, 'The one who had mercy on him.' Jesus told him, 'Go and do likewise'" (Luke 10:36–37). In the parables of divine mercy (Luke 15), Jesus speaks of the shepherd hoisting the lost sheep on his shoulders in jubilation and summoning all his friends to rejoice. The woman cries out, "Rejoice with me. I have found the silver piece I lost." Upon the return of the Prodigal Son, the father explains to the indignant elder son, "But we had to celebrate and rejoice!" The underlying theme of all three parables provides a striking insight into the mind of Jesus—"I tell you, there will be the same kind of joy before the angels of God over one repentant sinner" (Luke 15:10).

Jesus's gentleness with sinners flowed from his ability to read their hearts and to detect the sincerity and essential goodness there. Behind people's grumpiest poses or most puzzling defense mechanisms, behind their dignified airs, coarseness, or sneers, behind their silence or their curses, Jesus saw a little child who hadn't been loved enough and who had ceased growing because those around him had ceased believing in him. "In this sense," Adrian van Kaam writes, "Christ, and later the apostles, speak often about the faithful as children, no matter how tall, rich, clever, and successful they may be. For behind each one's strength is hiding a fallen person in need of redemption, a person precious in the eyes of God because of the unique treasure he is meant to be in time and eternity."

I have often seen Jesus Christ's delight over repentant sinners brought to life in the fellowship of Alcoholics Anonymous. The birthday celebrations marking the anniversary of an alcoholic's first, third, eighth, or twentieth year of sobriety resound with the merriment of the prodigal's return.

An old, broken man named Phil with three teeth in his mouth lived as a drunk on the streets for twenty years. Now he walks to the podium in a packed and quiet room. It's his first birthday. Nobody thought he'd make it. He starts to speak about once being lost and now being found. He suddenly chokes up and turns his back to the audience. A standing ovation starts. Men and women storm the podium. They kiss Phil on the lips, cheek, neck, and shoulders.

In his delightful little book *Off the Sauce*, Lewis Meyer writes:

> *If one could use only one word to describe the feeling of an AA meeting, it would be love. Love is the only word I know that encompasses friendship, understanding, sympathy, empathy, kindness, honesty, pride, and humility. The kind of love I mean is the kind Jesus had in mind when he said, "Love one another." Shoes might be shed, attention might be diverted, but there is a closeness between AAs, a closeness you seldom find anywhere. It is the only place I know where status means nothing. Nobody fools anybody else. Everyone is here because he or she made a slobbering mess of his or her life and is trying to put the pieces back together again. First things are first here. . . . I have attended thousands of church meetings, lodge meetings, brotherhood meetings—yet I have never found the kind of love I find at AA. For one small hour the high and mighty descend and the lowly rise. The leveling that results is what people mean when they use the word brotherhood.*

Christ's compassion is illuminated with astonishing clarity at the dinner given in the house of Simon the leper (Mark 14:3–9). Some of the guests become infuriated when a woman breaks an alabaster jar of precious perfume and begins pouring it over Jesus's head. "Leave her alone," Jesus commands. "Why are you bothering her?" He is so deeply moved by the woman's kindness that he wants it recounted and retold all over the world. "Write this down!" he tells them. "Until the end of time I want men to know how deeply this woman's love has affected me."

This statement is the long pent-up explosion of a love that can express itself at last, the secret of a heart pouring itself out. Jesus not only defends the woman's action but affirms her worth and acknowledges that he has been profoundly moved by her kindness. When we see the Master forgive the prostitute and nullify all her sins because of her great love (Luke 7:47), we glimpse God's joy in finding us again; we discover that this joy is capable of submerging all the evil we can commit. We can finally stop wondering about the past, the extent of our guilt, and the limits of God's love and mercy.

Loving Our Neighbors as Ourselves

Two curious phenomena dapple Christian life in America today. The first is our tendency to criticize more than compliment. Listen in on conversations in coffee shops, living rooms, and churches. Pay attention to the pundits and the newsmakers. We tend not only to begrudge the value of others but to appear downright sad when a person is praised. Many hypercritical Christians quickly deny the presence of any value anywhere and overemphasize the dark and ugly aspects of a person, situation, or institution at the expense of their noble and valuable facets. They delight in exposing the flaws and imperfections of others and glory in the absence of goodness. Senator William Fulbright of Arkansas once commented on this insidious tendency in the news media: "That Puritan self-righteousness which is never far below the surface of American life has broken through the frail barriers of civility and restraint, and the press has been in the vanguard of the new aggressiveness."

The target may be the national government, the local police force, or the coffee shop waitress. It matters little. The focus is on the limits of reality, on what a person or institution is not. Shortcomings and character defects are cause for celebration because they allow us to feel superior and even noble. On the day of my ordination my father said to me, "Remember that it's impossible to overestimate the worth of anyone." His words fly in the face of our tendency to underestimate the worth of everyone.

The second phenomenon is not unrelated to the first. It is what might be called the preponderance of the negative self-esteem. Self-esteem consists of how we see ourselves reflected in the eyes of others. This in turn conditions our perception of the world and our interaction with the community. As Christians, those of us with negative self-esteem see ourselves as basically unlovable. We negate our own worth, are haunted by feelings of inadequacy and inferiority, and close ourselves off from the value of others because they threaten our existence. The exaltation of another is experienced as a personal attack. When a colleague is appreciated, we become upset and irritable, belittle their motives as vainglorious, and decry the perniciousness of personality cults. We say to ourselves in effect: "I am a clod, a wrong person; I'm in the way, nobody cares." In group gatherings we feel like intruders. We sigh, "Nobody loves me."

Negative self-esteem would not be so damaging except for the fact that we interact with others in terms consistent with our own self-image. We select from reality only those aspects that confirm our own dim view of ourselves. We single out the dimension of a situation that points to rejection. In a simple conversation with someone close to us, their lack of enthusiasm confirms what we already suspect: "I am a bore." On the street we pass a person whom we value. He ignores us. That night when we go to bed we ignore the pleasant, even beautiful experiences of the day and instead go to sleep dwelling on the one incident that enhanced our negative self-portrait. Consequently, every such encounter becomes a total proof or disproof of our entire being. Every incident becomes a blanket condemnation of self and a reaffirmation of worthlessness.

In order to love our neighbors as ourselves, we must come to recognize our intrinsic worth and dignity and to love ourselves in the wholesome, appreciative way that Jesus commanded when he said, "Love your neighbor as yourself." The tendency to continually berate ourselves for real or imaginary failures, to belittle ourselves and underestimate our worth, to dwell exclusively on our dishonesty, self-centeredness, and lack of personal discipline, is the influence of our negative self-esteem. Reinforced by the critical feedback of our peers and the reproofs and humiliations of our community, we seem radically incapable of accepting, forgiving, or loving ourselves. In his opening address at the regional charismatic conference in Atlantic City, New Jersey, Father Francis McNutt touched an exposed nerve when he said, "If Jesus Christ has forgiven you all your sins and washed you in his own blood, what right do you have not to forgive yourself?"

The ability to love oneself is the root and foundation of our ability to love others and to love God. I can tolerate in others only what I can accept in myself. Van Kaam writes, "Gentleness toward my fragile precious self as called forth uniquely by God constitutes the core of gentleness with others and with the manifold created appearances of the Divine in my surroundings. It is also a main condition for my presence to God."

Ironically, our self-loathing too often leads us to damage the self-esteem of others. Andrew Greeley writes:

> *God's mission in the world and his mission in his relationship with the individual believer is essentially a mission of overcoming self-hatred. For self-hatred is a barrier to love. We hate other people not because we love ourselves too much but because we are not able to love ourselves enough. We fear and distrust them because we feel inadequate in our relationships to them; we hide behind anger and hatred because in some deep recess of our personality we do not think we are good enough for them.*

One night in New York City I was standing outside the Schubert Theater during the play's intermission. The tuxedoed gentlemen were in an intense discussion with the evening-gowned ladies on the influence of Schopenhauer on Samuel Beckett's *Theater of the Absurd*. I was about to deliver a timeless observation that would have precluded further discussion on the subject for at least a hundred years when an old woman peddling *Variety* newspapers approached. She was wearing sneakers and a cab driver's cap. I thrust a coin into her hand and snatched the paper. "Could I talk with you for a minute, Father?" she implored.

In those days I always wore the clerical collar. I knew I could not distinguish myself by my virtues, but I could by my clothing. I wore the Roman collar while taking a shower and placed it under my pajamas while I slept.

"Yes," I snapped, "just wait a minute."

As I turned around to my friends who were breathlessly awaiting my final riposte, I heard the old woman say, "Jesus wouldn't have talked to Mary Magdalene like that." She disappeared down the street.

The magnitude of what had happened hit me inside the theater. I had been so preoccupied with my own status that I treated the woman like a vending machine. I put a coin in her hand and out popped a magazine. I had shown no appreciation for the service she performed, no interest in her life, and an appalling lack of regard for her personal dignity. Preoccupation with my self-importance coupled with the failure to treat her with cordial love impregnated with respect for the sacredness of her unique personality only exacerbated her sense of worthlessness and further damaged her self-esteem. Her self-concept took shape in the way she saw herself reflected in the eyes of other people. If she came to church on Sunday and I was in the pulpit exhorting her to love God above all things . . . what hypocrisy from the man who helped undermine her ability to love anyone. A shriveled humanity has a shrunken capacity for receiving the rays of God's love.

The Compassion of Jesus

To think like Christ is to have Jesus's relational attitude toward his disciples. His attitude was beautifully expressed to me on a tour last fall through Sleepy Hollow Village on the Hudson River. Our guide's only instruction was, "Please be gentle with the lambs. They won't come to you if you frighten them."

When Jesus's eyes scanned the streets and hillsides, he felt compassion because the people were leaderless. He wept over Jerusalem. His words were not full of blaming and shaming, castigating and moralizing, accusing and guilt-inducing, ridiculing and belittling, threatening and bribing, evaluating and labeling. His mind was constantly inhabited by God's forgiveness. He took the initiative in seeking out sinners and justified his incredible ease and familiarity with them through the parables of divine mercy. The woman caught in adultery was not even asked if she was sorry. He did not demand a firm purpose of amendment. He did not lecture her on the harsh consequences of future infidelity. He saw her dignity as a human being destroyed by the self-righteous Pharisees. After reminding them of their solidarity in her sinfulness, he *looked* at the woman, loved her, forgave her, and told her not to sin anymore.

The French psychologist Marc Oraison writes, "To be loved is to be looked at in such a manner that the reality of recognition is disclosed." A Christian who doesn't merely see but looks at another communicates to that person that he is being recognized as a human being in an impersonal world of objects, as some*one* and not some-*thing*. If this simple psychological reality, difficult and demanding as it is, were actualized in human relationships, perhaps 98 percent of the obstacles to living like Jesus would be eliminated. For this is the very foundation of justice: the ability to recognize the other as a human being with the sign of the Lamb glowing on his brow.

The mere purchase of a postage stamp or a load of groceries at the supermarket can occasion an exchange of glances between clerk and customer capable of transforming a routine gesture into a true human encounter that is mutually ennobling. Words are unnecessary in this interaction for the Christian who knows the fundamental secret of Jesus in relation to his disciples: his sovereign respect for their dignity. They are people, not toys, functions, or occasions for personal compensation. In Luke's account of the Passion, he notes that after Peter's third denial of Jesus, "the Lord turned and *looked straight at Peter*" (Luke 22:61). In that look, the reality of recognition is disclosed. Peter knows that no one has ever loved him as Jesus does. The man whom he has confessed as the Christ, the Son of the living God, looks into his eyes, sees the transparent terror there, watches him act out the dreadful drama of his security addiction, and loves him.

The love of Jesus for Peter lay in his complete and unconditional acceptance of him. We who so automatically place conditions on our love ("If you really loved me you would . . . ") fail to see that this is an exchange, not unconditional love. (We tack on one of our addictions to finish the sentence.)

In Jesus's reaction to Peter we see that no man was ever freer of pressures, conventions, or addictions. Jesus was so liberated from the dominating barrage of desires, demands, expectations, needs, and inflexible emotional programming that he could accept the unacceptable. He did not have to resort to screams, vicious attacks, or undue threats. He communicated his deepest feelings to Peter by a look. And that look transformed and re-created Peter: "He went outside and wept bitterly" (Luke 22:62).

Compassion means that when you empathize with the predicament of another person, you send out the signal, "Yes, I know. I've been there too." You experience the situation from that person's position. To be compassionate is to understand the conflicts other people have created in themselves without getting caught up in their poignant drama; you realize your compassion will be most effective if you stay centered in loving acceptance. As Jesus saw Peter playing out his addiction, and suffering because of it, he remained profoundly attuned to the humanity and dignity of the man. His transparent look imbued with

God's forgiveness not only brought Peter to tears but enabled him to continue his journey onward and upward into a richer life with Christ.

A few days later the Risen Jesus would say to the same man: "'I tell you the truth, when you were younger you dressed yourself and went where you wanted; but when you are old you will stretch out your hands, and someone else will dress you and lead you to where you do not want to go.' Jesus said this to indicate the kind of death by which Peter would glorify God. Then he said to him, 'Follow me'" (John 21:18–19). This time there was no denial or complaint. Peter accepted what had been previously unacceptable. Years later this same man would write: "Love each other deeply, because love covers over a multitude of sins" (1 Peter 4:8). In the light of his own painful growth, he tells the Gentile Christians, "Like newborn babies, crave pure spiritual milk so that by it you may grow up in your salvation" (1 Peter 2:2).

Peter's betrayal of the Master, like so many of our own moral relapses and refusals to walk with the Lord, was not a terminal failure but an occasion for painful personal growth into the person God intended he be. Is it unrealistic to assume that years later Peter praised God for the servant girl who turned him into a sniveling coward in Caiphas's courtyard?

Jesus was not in the business of reinforcing negative self-concepts. "The bruised reed he will not crush; the smoldering wick he will not quench" (Matthew 12:20). He was merciless only with those who showed contempt for human dignity; he had no compassion for those who laid intolerable burdens on the backs of others and refused to carry them themselves. He unmasked the illusions and superficial good intentions of the Pharisees for what they were and called them hypocrites, "a brood of vipers" (Matthew 12:34). He had no mercy for those who showed no mercy and an utter lack of compassion for the uncompassionate.

To live and think as Jesus did is to discover the sincerity, goodness, and truth often hidden behind the gross, coarse exteriors of our fellow human beings. It is to see the good in others that they don't see in themselves and to affirm this good in the face of powerful evidence to the contrary. It is not a blind optimism that ignores the reality of evil but a perspective that acknowledges the good so repeatedly and so insistently that the wayward must eventually respond in agreement.

In the man Jesus, the mind of God becomes transparent. There is nothing of self to be seen, only the unconditional love of God. Jesus lays bare the Ground of man's being in his encounter with Peter in the courtyard.

The axis of the Christian moral revolution is love (Jesus called it the sign by which the disciple would be recognized). The danger lurks in our subtle attempts to minimize, rationalize, and justify our moderation in this regard. Turning the other cheek, walking the extra mile, offering no resistance to injury, being reconciled with one another, and forgiving seventy times seven times are not arbitrary whims of the Savior. He did not preface the Sermon on the Mount with, "It would be nice if. . . ." His "new" commandment structures the new covenant in his blood. So central is the precept of love that Paul called it the fulfillment of the Law.

"Reason demands moderation in love as in all things; faith destroys moderation here," writes John McKenzie. "Faith tolerates a moderate love of one's fellow man no more than it tolerates a moderate love between God and man." The commandment of love is the entire Christian moral code. Thomas Merton stated that a "good" Christian who harbors hatred in his heart toward any person or ethnic group is objectively an apostate from the Christian faith.

Learning to Think Like Christ: One Story

In the early stages of Alcoholics Anonymous, there was considerable discussion and debate over the qualifications for membership. What were the rules for admission? Could certain individuals be excluded, as from a country club? Who would get in, and who would be left out? Who would determine whether an alcoholic was deserving or undeserving? Some lobbied to limit membership to persons of "moral responsibility"; others insisted that the only dues to be paid would be the personal admission, "I think I am an alcoholic. I want to stop drinking."

The debate was resolved in a most unusual way. The story is related in the book *Twelve Steps and Twelve Traditions,* whose authors naturally remain anonymous. It affords a remarkable insight into Christ-like compassion and admirably sums up what I have been trying to say in this chapter.

On the AA calendar it was year two. The organization consisted of two struggling, nameless groups of alcoholics trying to hold their faces up to the light.

A newcomer appeared at a meeting of one of these groups, knocked at the door, and asked to be let in. He talked frankly with the group's oldest member. He soon proved that his was a desperate case and that above all he wanted to get well. "But," he asked, "will you let me join your group? Since I'm the victim of another addiction even more stigmatized than alcoholism, you may not want me among you. Or will you?"

The oldest member summoned two others and in confidence lay the explosive facts on their laps. Said he, "Well, what about it? If we turn this man away, he'll soon die. If we let him in, only God knows what trouble he'll brew. What should the answer be—yes or no?"

At first the elders could only look at the objections. "We deal with alcoholics only. Shouldn't we sacrifice this one for the sake of the many?" So went the discussion while the newcomer's fate hung in the balance.

Then one of the three spoke in a very different tone. "What we are really afraid of," he said, "is our reputation. We are much more afraid of what people might say than the trouble this strange alcoholic might bring. As we've been talking, five short words have been running through my mind. Something keeps repeating to me, 'What would the Master do?'"

Not another word was said.

6.

The Work of
the Kingdom

Jesus Christ is not only the center of the gospel but the whole gospel. The four evangelists never focus on another personality. Marginal characters remain on the periphery, and no one else is allowed to take center stage. Various individuals are introduced only to interrogate, respond to, or react to Jesus. Nicodemus, the Samaritan woman, Peter, Thomas, Caiphas, Pilate, and scores of others are secondary to the person of Jesus. This is as it should be, for the New Testament is a vision of salvation. When the final curtain falls, Jesus will upstage all the famous, beautiful, and powerful people who have ever lived. Every man and woman will be seen as responding to Jesus. As T. S. Eliot put it, "O my soul, be prepared to meet him who knows how to ask questions."

In the man Jesus there is an utter single-mindedness toward God. But more than knowledge and heart connection is involved; Jesus lives in order to shed light on the reign of God and life in God's kingdom.

"My food," said Jesus, "is to do the will of him who sent me and to finish his work." (John 4:34)

The words I say to you are not my own. Rather, it is the Father, living in me, who is doing his work. (John 14:10)

Father, if you are willing, take this cup from me; yet not my will, but yours be done. (Luke 22:42)

And in the temple Jesus tersely replies to his mother, "Why were you searching for me? Didn't you know I had to be in my Father's house?" (Luke 2:49).

Another passage is even more basic. Jesus is teaching and surrounded by a group of listeners. Someone nudges him: "Your mother and your brothers are outside looking for you." And he, who knew so well who his mother was, answered from the very depths from which he drew his life: "Who are my mother and my brothers?" He paused, looked around at those seated in the circle, and continued. "Here are my mother and my brothers! Whoever does God's will is my brother and sister and mother" (Mark 3:31–35).

We must not allow these words to be interpreted as allegory. The will of God is reality. It is like a river of life coming down from God to Jesus—a bloodstream from which he draws life even more profoundly and more powerfully than he drew life from his mother. And whoever is ready to do the will of God becomes a part of this bloodstream. The believer and doer is united to the life of Christ Jesus even more truly, deeply, and strongly than Jesus was united to his mother. Here we find an utter lack of human sentimentality in Jesus. The two focal points of his ministry are God and himself. Again, this is as it should be.

The mind of Jesus is focused on the fulfillment of God's will through the proclamation of the Reign of God. Jesus's intimacy with God and awareness of God's holiness fill him with an all-consuming thirst for the things of God. His interior life of trust and loving surrender is not simply a matter of personal prayer, private religious experience, and delight in God's intimate presence. Such a limited relationship with God would ignore the real world and its struggle for redemption, justice, and peace. No, the inner life of Jesus Christ takes expression in a special, vital quality of presence in the world in the most active situations.

There was a towering desire within Jesus to reveal his Father in serving the poor, the captive, the blind, and all who were in need. Jesus was entirely devoured by this mission. It was Jesus's experience of God's holiness that created the imperative of preaching the reign of God's justice, peace, and forgiving love.

Jesus ordered his life around this mission, forgoing the comforts of stability and permanence: "Foxes have holes and birds of the air their nests, but the Son of Man has no place to lay his head" (Luke 9:58). He never lingered long in one place. When the disciples looked for him, he responded, "I must preach the good news of the kingdom of God to the other towns also, because that is why I was sent" (Luke 4:43). Others might have stayed behind, preoccupied with security, pleasure, and power, but Jesus went on without stopping, always driven by the kingdom vision.

"The relationship of Jesus with His disciples can be understood only in the context of His mission," writes José Comblin. Jesus did not concern himself with the families of his disciples or with the families of friends and colleagues. When one disciple asked to take time for a family burial, Jesus replied, "Let the dead bury their own dead, but you go and proclaim the kingdom of God" (Luke 9:60).

When Jesus received the baptism of John at the Jordan River, he had a core identity experience. The heavens were split, the Spirit descended in the form of a dove, and Jesus heard the voice of his Father, "You are my Son, whom I love; with you I am well pleased"

(Luke 3:22). The synoptic Gospels ascribe the identification of Jesus as "the servant of Yahweh" directly to God. Whatever the external trappings, Jesus learned at the Jordan in a decisive inner experience that he was Son, Servant, and Beloved of the Father. George Aschenbrenner says, "This clear, core identity experience results from, brings and celebrates his profound intimacy with his Father."

The temptations in the desert challenged the authenticity of the Jordan experience. All three of Satan's ploys ("If you are the Son . . . ") are intended to press the same questions: Is Jesus really Son-Servant-Beloved? Was the Jordan experience merely an illusion? Did anyone else hear the voice Jesus heard? Satan launches a frontal assault on the religious identity of Jesus. The gospel periscope does not dwell on the inner struggle and fierce conflict in the human heart of Jesus, but the issue was tumultuous. Aschenbrenner notes, "He is asked here in risk and trust to ratify, and thus to embrace, at the level of mission and action, his own relation to the Father." In the starkness and simplicity of the vast uncluttered wilderness, Jesus interpreted his existence and his mission in the world at a new and decisive level and emerged from the desert with the Breath of God on his face.

It should not be assumed, however, that his time of testing is over. Luke says, "When the devil had finished all this tempting, he left him until an opportune time"

(4:13). Jesus's trust in his Father is not a single decision that leaves him certain of his mission and immune to the Tempter. His brush with the devil in the desert is the first of a series of challenges to his self-awareness and inner identity as Son-Servant-Beloved of the Father. The enduring temptation of his ministry is to fulfill his mission in a way that runs counter to God's agenda. He could begin with a flashy demonstration of power by turning stones into bread and end with a sensational exhibition of might, coming down from the cross to exact revenge on God's enemies. The allure of cultivating security, pleasure, and power is Satan's worldly way. Jesus utterly rejects it.

In the final foolishness of love, Jesus freely accepts death on the cross. It is the ultimate act of trust, the climax of a life lived in God. Jesus knows who he is. On the deepest level of his existence, Jesus reaffirms his position as Son-Servant-Beloved of the Father and fulfills his mission. Jesus's death on the cross gives final, definitive, and everlasting form to his spiritual identity and to his intimate, loving trust in God. John Shea notes: "God raised Jesus from the dead not because he never flinched, talked back, or questioned but having flinched, talked back, and questioned, He remained faithful."

Jesus's self-awareness and unflagging zeal in his ministry must be seen in direct and unceasing relation to his interior life of growing intimacy with the Father.

We must not lose sight of this logical link: the primacy of mission and his consuming zeal for proclaiming the kingdom of God derive not from theological reflection, the desire to edify others, trendy spirituality, or a loose sense of goodwill toward the world. Its wellspring is God's holiness and Jesus's self-awareness of his relation to God.

It is highly significant that the gospel is punctuated with numerous references to Jesus's withdrawal from the mainstream of activity to pray. The Bible indicates that Jesus needs this special kind of intimate contact with his Father. His own interior growth and sense of mission and direction depend very much on these times of prayer. Shea says, "It is admittedly guesswork (but not gratuitous guesswork) to surmise that Jesus went to the mountains to pray not because He was in lockstep toward the kingdom but because he had to recommit his freedom to the trust God had given him."

The heart of God is Jesus's hiding place, a strong protective space where God is near, where connection is renewed, where trust, love, and self-awareness never die but are continually rekindled. In times of opposition, rejection, hatred, and danger, Jesus retreats to that hiding place where he is loved. In times of weakness and fear, a gentle strength and mighty perseverance are born there. In the face of mounting incomprehension and mistrust, the Father alone understands him. "No one knows who the Son is except the Father . . . " (Luke

10:22). The Pharisees plot secretly to destroy him, fair-weather friends shift their allegiance, one disciple denies him, and another betrays him, but nothing can remove Jesus from his Father's love. In the seclusion of desert places, he meets with El Shaddai, and what those moments mean to him can scarcely be understood. But this much can be said: the primary, growing, definitive identity of Jesus as his Father's Son, Servant, and Beloved is profoundly reinforced there. Nothing must interfere with proclaiming the good news of eternal life and helping people move into a way of life that will enable them to grow toward eternity—a way of peace and justice with room for human dignity to be recognized and for love to blossom.

So essential is this connection that Jesus encourages his disciples to take up the same practice of rest and respite. Upon the disciples' jubilant return from the active ministry, Jesus counsels them in preserving their humanness and centering in their self-awareness: "'Come with me by yourselves to a quiet place and get some rest.' So they went away by themselves in a boat to a solitary place" (Mark 6:31–32).

It is important to keep these times of withdrawal in the context and rhythm of Jesus's very active and busy life. Such moments of prayer are always oriented to his presence in the world. The major decisions of his life (for example, the selection of the twelve who will enter the intimate circle of his friendship and share in his mission) are always preceded by a night alone on the mountaintop. And of course there is his tortured night in the Garden of Gethsemane spent pleading for the strength to do the will of his Father.

One cannot but think of the number of wrong marriages, wrong jobs, wrong personal relationships, and all the concomitant suffering that would be avoided if Christians submitted their decision-making process to the Lordship of Jesus Christ and shared in his intimate trust in God's direction. We often forget that we have the same access to God that Jesus enjoyed. But we must never forget that our Creator cares. God knows each of us by name and is deeply involved in the dramas of our personal existence. "Indeed, the very hairs of your head are all numbered" (Luke 12:7). Within this climate of trust we can confidently search to discern the will of God. It is the atmosphere in which all our decisions become clear and from which all our actions spring. The outcome is less vague, ambiguous, and uncertain than we might suppose. The sounds of inner peace resonate in the heart attuned to God, while the untuned heart caught up in singing its own song throbs with agitation, conflict, dissonance, and contretemps.

In considering what it means for us to put on the mind of Christ, we can easily distance ourselves from Jesus's preoccupation with his mission—he was, after all, the Messiah, the Sent One. He was sinless and had none of the distractions of family, work, and modern life to stand in the way of his calling. But rather than succumb to those distractions, we can find hope by following Christ's example of single-minded devotion to the things of God.

The Divided Self

Jesus always seemed to know who he was. Throughout his life there was a developing awareness of his person and mission, but he always had a coherent sense of self. His habitual self-awareness and unwavering fidelity to his mission stand in contrast to how we live in contemporary American society. A lifestyle centered on security, pleasure, and power precludes the possibility of establishing any coherent sense of self for the simple reason that these desires peremptorily exclude God.

Just as the mind of Christ Jesus created his world, so too do our minds create our worlds. An ego grasping for security, pleasure, and power freely barters self-awareness for something that will enhance the mirage of fulfillment that these desires bring. Our addictive patterns—our expectations, desires, attachments, demands, and mental models—dominate our perception of self, others, and the world. This grasping, manipulative focus keeps us on that roller-coaster ride of pleasure and disappointment that makes continuity of character and fidelity to vision impossible.

Paul calls this desire-driven life *sarx*—life in the flesh. Here our mental and emotional programming inclines us to be controlled by the need to get enough from the world to feel secure, propels us to find happiness through more and better pleasurable experiences, and directs our attention to dominating people and situations, thereby increasing our prestige and power.

The crisis of American spirituality, put bluntly, is Spirit versus flesh. The failure or flat refusal to abide in the mind of Christ creates duality and separation within us. We do not choose decisively between God and Mammon, and our procrastination constitutes a decision itself. We carefully distribute ourselves between flesh and Spirit with a watchful eye on both. The unwillingness to sustain ourselves with the awareness that we are children of God causes a spiritual schizophrenia of the most frightening kind. It is not that I am afraid to tell you who I am; I truly cannot tell you because I don't know myself who I am. I have not given the deep inner assent to my Christian identity. I am afraid of losing my life if I were to find my real self. God calls me by my name, and I do not answer because I do not know my name.

The lifestyle of schizoid Christians is erratic because at different moments we deliberately separate ourselves from our real selves. We hug certain events, experiences, and relationships to ourselves and exclude the presence of the indwelling Spirit. It may be a movie, a conversation, an illicit love affair, or a business transaction. Later, we re-enter the self that calls itself Christian and take part in events where God is celebrated in speech and song. Afterward we confide to friends, "Worship was kind of flat tonight."

Heightened by what someone has called "the agnosticism of inattention"—the lack of personal discipline to overcome media bombardment, sterile conversation, and utilitarian relationships—our self-awareness grows dim, the presence of a loving God fades into the distance and the possibility of trust and intimacy seems less plausible. Inattentiveness to the holy destroys openness to the Spirit. Just as the failure to be attentive dissolves personal love in a human relationship, so inattention to the real self dissolves loving awareness of the divine relationship. A verdant heart becomes a devastated vineyard. It is impossible to consider God with heart and head filled with earthly business.

When we periodically close ourselves off from God, our hearts are touched by the icy finger of agnosticism. Christian agnosticism does not consist so much in the denial of a personal God as in the unbelief of inattention to the sacred. The way we live bears unmistakable witness to our *loving awareness* or lack of it.

Life in the Spirit implies the existential knowledge of being loved by God and sharing Jesus's own experience of that love. But so many of the things we do in our solitary moments have nothing to do with the Spirit or with the living will of God. Bothered by this dichotomy, we plunge into spiritual activities and get involved in church-related organizations and events in an effort to fill the empty space we know needs filling. Disinclined to renounce managerial control of our lives and unwilling to run the risk of living in union with Yahweh, we seek personal security and reassurance in rituals, devotions, liturgies, and prayer meetings. These structures provide a modicum of peace and promise that the comfortable piety and material possessions that constitute the sense of self will not be disturbed.

There is a need for careful discernment here. The evidence of earnestness, sincerity, and effort is considerable. But something is missing.

That something is transparency. The glory shining on the face of Christ Jesus does not shine in many of us. Unlike Jesus, we have not given our deep inner assent to who we are meant to be. We have not surrendered to the mystery of the fire of the Spirit that burns within. We stand close enough to the fire to stay warm, but we never plunge in; nor do we come out burned and incandescently transformed. We might be nicer than most other people or have better morals, but we do not live as *brand-new creations*. Instead, our opaque personalities reveal our divided hearts.

Living in the Kingdom

The only possible way to move out of our obsessive self-awareness and into the life of Christ is to surrender ourselves and let God be God. Such a surrender involves mining the field of our hearts and searching for this pearl of God's truth hidden deep within us: we belong to God. This precious discovery makes security, pleasure, and power look like cheap, painted fragments of glass. "I consider [all things] rubbish, that I may gain Christ" (Philippians 3:8).

In claiming ownership of our divine status as sons and daughters of the Creator of the Universe, we gain a coherent sense of self. We lose ourselves to find ourselves. This loss paves the way for the Holy Spirit to transform our lives. No longer stuck in the flesh, we begin to understand what Paul meant when he said, "It is for freedom that Christ set us free" (Galatians 5:1).

This loving awareness of being the child of the Father moves us out of a life spent pursuing our base desires and frees us to pursue the kingdom of God. We no longer have to live lives bifurcated by our needs. Everything we have and are forms but one self, one heart beating with the lifeblood of Jesus. There can be no firmness of character or consistency of conduct without this courageous act of self-affirmation. Paul said, "I no longer live, but Christ lives in me" (Galatians 2:20). Therein lies transparency.

With the veil lifted, much of the emotional suffering caused by our addictive desires is healed. We can begin to drop all of our manipulative games—the money game, the security game, the male-female game, the power game, the knowledge game, the expert game, and so on. We can present ourselves simply to others: "Here I am. It's all I've got." In humble self-awareness and sovereign freedom we can truly *be* for others without fear of rejection or concern for their usefulness to us.

One night at Coney Island a group of us were standing in front of a restaurant eating hot dogs and drinking beer. A few yards away, in the center of the sidewalk, a black man was pouring a can of beer on the head and down the blouse of a pregnant white girl. She couldn't have been more than fifteen years old. He was describing in lurid detail how he had sexually abused her in the past and what he had in mind for later. She started to cry.

Someone in our group looked at this scene in disgust and said, "Let's get out of here."

We started toward the car when, like a bell sounding deep within my soul, I heard, "Who are you?"

I stopped as if my shoes were glued to the pavement. "I am the son of my Father," I answered.

"That is my daughter," came the reply.

I went back, drew the girl aside, and spoke with her for several minutes. Some spectators began to shout at me and call me vulgar names. That night I wept—not for the crowd or even for the girl but for myself. I wept for the countless times I had played the silent sentinel, afraid to acknowledge who I am, unable to recognize the least of my sisters. I saw her dignity being degraded and was content to walk away. I had violated my own identity: "Anyone, then, who knows the good he ought to do and doesn't do it, sins" (James 4:17).

So often we are self-moved and self-motivated rather than moved and motivated by the Spirit. When our sense of self is derived from our base desires, we act in ways intended to win approval, avoid criticism, or escape rejection. Dietrich Bonhoeffer wrote:

> Satan's desire is to turn me in on myself to the extent that I become enslaved and become a destructive force in community. The thrust from Jesus Christ is the opposite—to enhance my freedom so that I can become a creative force of love. It is the spirit of self-centeredness and selfishness versus the spirit of openness and self-sacrifice for the good of others.

The cure for our selfishness is to develop discerning hearts. When we put on the mind of Christ and focus our thinking and behavior on the kingdom of God, we can begin to evaluate our choices, our decisions, and our motivations with new clarity. We move from a place of sleepwalking through our lives and being driven by our most earthbound instincts to a place of living in full consciousness of our position as heirs of the most High God. George Maloney writes:

> We used to peg people we didn't like as conservatives if we were liberal, liberals if we were conservative. Another convenient grouping of people was the younger and older generations. Today I feel the real difference that separates humans is the difference between persons (young and old) who live predominantly on a sensory level and others who live on a level of greater expanded consciousness. The first group is the object at which the typical American advertisement on TV is aimed. Such value above all else, body comfort, no pain, to eat and sleep well, body beauty and physical health. The second group embraces the smaller segment of humanity that is pushing always toward a greater synthesis of knowledge, a greater experience of the unified meaning of life with man's directing all his energies toward that ultimacy.

In some ways, this process of focusing our lives on the mind and work of Jesus involves distancing ourselves from the world around us in an effort to break away from our dysfunctions and addictions. To them we appear foolish and misguided. Thus this kind of focus cannot happen without a daily—even hourly—decision to surrender to the sway of the Spirit. Ralph Martin says:

> *Very soon in a serious life of faith we must renounce our bondage to darkness, we must be freed from our attachment to those things that hold us back from a pure surrender to the action of God in us. We must live out totally those renunciations we made in our baptism and which we ratify at every Easter Vigil. And it is here we find great difficulty, and meet with the obstacles of selfishness, sensuality, ambition, resentment, pride, fear, etc.*

Christians often speak of the necessity of submitting ourselves to God. But there is an essential difference between submission and surrender. The former is the conscious acceptance of reality. There is a superficial yielding, but tension continues. I say that I accept who I am, but I do not accept it so fully that I am willing to actually *act out* who I am. It is halfhearted acceptance. It is described by such words as *resignation, compliance, acknowledgment, concession.* There remains a feeling of reservation, a tug in the direction of non-acceptance. Surrender, on the other hand, is the moment when my forces of resistance cease to function, when I cannot help but respond to the call of the

Spirit. "The emotional state of surrender," writes Dr. Harry S. Tiebout, "is a state in which there is a persisting capacity to accept reality. It is a state that is really positive and creative."

The ability to surrender is a gift of God. However eagerly we may desire it, however diligently we may strive to acquire it, surrender cannot be attained by personal endeavor. "With respect to the act of surrender, let me emphasize this point," Tiebout writes. "It is an unconscious event, not willed by the patient even if he should desire to do so."

And yet the intensity of our desire does matter. Our dedication to growth is the single most important determinant of our spiritual development. Without an intense inner commitment, we are little more than dilettantes playing spiritual games. The pearl of great price—the mind of Christ—must be the most treasured value in our lives, and we must seek it in persevering prayer, in sacramental healing, and in the strength of the Christian community. Only then will the miracle of transparency, love, and oneness unfold in our lives. "If you then, though you are evil, know how to give good gifts to your children, how much more will your Father in heaven give the Holy Spirit to those who ask him" (Luke 11:13). It is God's will that we grow in holiness (1 Thessalonians 4:7), know the truth that makes us free (John 8:32), and rejoice with a joy that no one can take from us (John 16:22).

The Kingdom and the World

The living awareness of his Father's goodness and love created the imperative of mission in the heart of Jesus and consumed him with zeal for his Father's house (John 2:17). To think like Jesus is to experience being loved so completely by God that we are existentially incapable of being other than the children of the Father in Christ Jesus. It is overwhelmingly joyful news, and we become overwhelmingly joyful people because of it. We cannot contain it because love by its nature is meant to be shared. We realize that all men and women are loved in the same way but recognize that many are unaware of it. They are locked into loneliness, fear, alienation, apathy, and ignorance. No one has told them of all the things that happened in Jerusalem; they are like sheep without a shepherd.

Robert DeNiro's stunning performance in the film *Taxi Driver* captures this mood forcefully. He plays Travis Bickle, a taxi driver who doesn't know who he is, where he's going, or why he's living. He seeks out a veteran cabbie for advice. "Don't take yourself so seriously," he's told. "Get drunk and get laid. That's all there is. You're only a taxi driver." How many of our brothers and sisters wander through their days with this same sense of purposelessness, of being orphans in the world. What a gift we can be to the world when we are transparent answers to their most heartfelt questions!

In the face of the loneliness and pain we see in our neighbors, we simply cannot shutter the doors and say, "I'll stay in my own little world, safe and serene in God's loving presence." Our awareness of God becomes the birthplace of a consuming zeal and a towering desire to "tell it on the mountain." We are driven by the Spirit to proclaim by word and example the peace, justice, and forgiving love of God. Perhaps by nothing more (or less) than our friendship extended to another, a friendship that is real, unselfish, nonproselytizing, without condescension, and full of profound respect, we can lead another to discover, "I too am loved by my Father in the Lord Jesus." It is the loving awareness of God's holiness revealed in Jesus Christ coupled with a deep compassion for redeemed humanity that creates the imperative of Christian mission.

A friend of mine once wrote:

To be a son of the Father, like Jesus, is really to delight in this relationship and to fully embrace this identity. It is to enjoy thoroughly and take great pride in finding myself so situated. It is to sense the extraordinary privilege that is mine through no merit of my own. It is to appreciate in a very human sense the dignity of the title bestowed on me and to walk with my head held high. It is to have the aristocratic bearing of one born to royalty. It is to envy no man anything, for my privileged position transcends all comparisons, eclipses all worldly honors and titles, and fills my cup with a joy beyond all telling.

What is my Father like? One day he grew so apprehensive that I might fail to understand how loving and wise, gentle and powerful he is, that He sent me a complete and perfect expression of himself in his Son Jesus. Everything my Father has, he entrusted to Jesus so that in looking at Jesus, I can see and know my Father. Let me tell you the most beautiful and thrilling thing he ever said to me. I wake up to it each morning and lay there sleepy, dazed, and happy because I always hear it as for the first time. "As the Father has loved me, so do I love you."

Christ's relationship with his Father and his attendant focus on the things of God moves him to a place where his deepest desire is for all things and all people to find oneness under God. This desire is reflected in the "high priestly prayer" of Jesus in the Cenacle:

That all of them may be one, Father, just as you are in me and I am in you. May they also be in us so that the world may believe that you sent me. I have given them the glory that you gave me, that they may be one as we are one: I in them and you in me. May they

be brought to complete unity to let the world know
that you sent me and have loved them even as you
have loved me. (John 17:21–23)

There is in this prayer a marvelous call for oneness between the created order and its Creator. If we want to think as Jesus did, we too must break through our illusions of separation from others. While we make a conscious effort to live apart from the worries of the world, we must also recognize that God created a world saturated with beauty, lucidity, vividness, and intensity. This recognition is an essential element of living in the kingdom of God. George Maloney writes:

Whatever the person is doing—opening or closing his
eyes, he finds the Divine Presence everywhere in the
unity of all things, and this forces the person out of
himself in a spirit of worship and service. . . . It is an
experience of God at the heart of all matter. He loves
this being, this person, this tree, this stone, and God
at the same time. There is no moving from this to
that, but in his vision he sees at one and the same
time the created being and the infinite love of God
who creates this being and gives it to him as a gift.
He finds the gift and the Giver in the same look.

The culture in which we live makes much of the concept of boundaries, of separating ourselves from others for the sake of mental health. In theory, this concept allows us to live in such a way that we resist letting the dysfunctions of others alter the way we want to live our own lives. Much of what we've discussed here could fit nicely into a discussion of boundaries and learning to live without worrying about the expectations of others. Yet in our self-centered desires we have twisted the notion of boundaries to serve as an excuse for ignoring the needs of others. We have allowed the setting of boundaries to become not a tool for growth but a barrier to relationships.

Christ's call for unity demands that we move beyond an isolationist sense of personal boundaries and the limits usually associated with self-motivated behavior. No longer can I look at others as people with whom I have no connection. Instead, unity in God calls me to experience all people and things as extensions of God's family, of which I am a part. There is no boundary between the part of God that lives in me and the part that lives in all of creation.

In this state, Ken Keyes Jr. writes,

> *you can function with enormous effectiveness*
> *because you have lost the addictive screens that limit*
> *your receptiveness. You are now tuned to the finer*
> *vibrations of all the people and the world around*
> *you. You are open to the broad spectrum of all the*

finer cues that the world around you has been
sending you all the time which you were previously
unable to pick up, for your consciousness has been
occupied.

The life of Francis of Assisi offers a fine insight into what it means to live in unity with God's creation. His words and gestures are the manifestation of a heart completely surrendered to God. Francis understood that the beauty of sensate things is the voice by which they announce God. "It is you who made me beautiful, not I, but you." At the moment Francis discovered what created things conceal, Creation cried aloud to him. It was his reflection upon them and the attention paid them that opened their voices to cry, "How beautiful is the one who made us!" In chatting amiably with the birds, scolding the wolf of Gubbio for disturbing the neighborhood, keeping a lamb at the Portiuncula to remind the brothers of the Lamb of God, and writing a lyrical canticle to Brother Sun, Francis communed with God in nature and revealed a cosmic consciousness of surpassing sensitivity.

Above all, it was through his gestures that Francis mirrored the transparent beauty of his spirit. One rainy morning he approached the piazza where the village church was located. A crowd followed him chanting, "Santo, Santo, holy one." The villagers knew that the local priest had not been living a life of moral rectitude. As Francis reached the piazza, the curate happened to come out of the church. The crowd watched in tense silence. What would Francis do? Denounce the priest for the scandal he had caused? Sermonize the villagers on the nature of human frailty and the need for compassion? Simply ignore the priest and continue on his way? Francis stepped forward, knelt in the mud, took the priest's hand, and kissed it. That was all. "The splendor of a just soul," wrote Thomas Aquinas, "is so seductive that it surpasses the beauty of all sensible things."

A remarkable thing happens when we embrace our unity with all of God's creation: *everything we have given up is given back*. Our worries concerning security, pleasure, and power fall away in the recognition that all is well in the kingdom of God. The teaching of Jesus, "Enough, then, of worrying about tomorrow. Let tomorrow take care of itself" (Matthew 6:34), is no mere moral maxim but a personal reality at the lived level of daily experience. In this context, the author Murray Bodo writes of Francis:

And he was not worried or anxious about yesterday, today or tomorrow because Christ is, and all things are in Him and He is in the Father. Francis no longer worried, not because he was a naive optimist, but

*because he had become in prayer and penance a realist
who saw the unimportance of everything but God,
and in God and with Him and through Him, the
importance of everything. God was everywhere and
His presence charged creation with a power and a
glory that made everything shine with goodness and
beauty in Francis' eyes. God's touch on everything
inspirited everything that was.*

Everything given up is given back and experienced
in a new way through the transforming power of the
indwelling Spirit. Security, pleasure, and power are at
the service of love and are integrated into the total
Christian personality. The spiritual schizophrenia that
has absorbed so much time and drained so much
strength ceases. An immense amount of energy is now
available for the building of the kingdom. The unremit-
ting peace and joy that flow from union with God and
God's world are the triumphant fruits of the Holy Spirit
and the goal of the Christian pilgrimage. They are
available to us on the same terms that Francis won them:
perfect detachment. "Everything Francis saw or heard
or smelled or breathed was his, because nothing was
his," observes Bodo. "He had fiercely rooted out of his
heart all possessiveness and greed, and as Jesus had
promised, *all these things were given back to him,* pressed
down and overflowing with love."

Justice

In 1975 the theologian George Lindbeck said:

*We are now, so it is generally said, in the midst
of changes as great as any in the two millennia of
Christian history. A successful revolution in
traditional terms of thought and life is as badly
needed as at any time in the past. We are confronted
with innumerable and often contradictory proposals
as to the direction that change should take. For some,
to mention just two examples, it is that of the
charismatic movement, and for others, that of
theologies of liberation.*

Thirty years later, the worldview of those who see
with the eyes and mind of Christ continues to be a win-
some wedding between personal spirituality and liberation theology. With Jesus we long for the unity of the
global community, the dawning of the day when the lion
will lie down with the lamb, East and West will know each
other's language, black and white will really communicate, cities of apathy and despair will experience the sun-
shine of a better life, and all men and women will rejoice
in the Spirit that makes us one. The sense of oneness with
the created world and our own freedom in the Spirit and
the awareness that liberation and liberty are the nucleus of

the message of Jesus direct our attention to the emancipation of the world. We cannot claim to have the mind of Christ and remain insensitive to the oppression of our brothers and sisters. We cannot stay oblivious to the world's struggle for redemption, freedom, and peace. We know that the good done to the poor—the least of our brothers and sisters (Matthew 25:40)—is done to Jesus himself. We know that we must commit ourselves to concrete action on behalf of liberation. There are things to be done. The theologian Enrique Dussel writes:

> *The person who sees a free Other in the poor and liberates the slave from Egypt is the person who truly loves God, for the slave in Egypt is the very epiphany of God himself. If a person opens up to the slave in Egypt, he opens up to God; if he shuts out the slave in Egypt, he shuts out God. The person who does not commit himself to the liberation of the slaves in Egypt is an atheist. He is Cain killing Abel. Once Abel was dead, Cain was alone. He now believed himself to be the only one, the Eternal. He presented himself as a pantheistic god. That was the temptation posed to Adam in the garden: "You will be like gods." To be like God is to pretend to be the one and only being; to refuse to open up to the Other, who has been murdered.*
>
> *God, however, keeps on revealing himself to us as the Other who summons us. He is the first Other. If I*

*do not listen to my fellow man in bondage, then I am
not listening to God either. If I do not commit myself
to the liberation of my fellowman, then I am an athe-
ist. Not only do I not love God, I am actually fighting
against God because I am affirming my own divinity.*

What leads Christians to collaborate in the liberation of the oppressed is the conviction that the gospel
message is radically incompatible with an unjust, alien-
ated society. Many Christians have come to know Jesus
Christ in a personal way. He is the Savior who, by liberating us from sin, liberates us from the very root of
social injustice. His redemptive work embraces every
dimension of human existence. "The ongoing life of
the church as a process of liberation is an essential tenet
in Christian doctrine," notes Dussel. "It is embodied in
the notion of 'Passover' or 'pasch,' and the life of the
Church is a paschal one."

The fire of Pentecostal freedom must be cast upon
the darkness of oppressive and dehumanizing structures, institutions, and situations. The saving work of
Jesus Christ will remain unfinished until it is kindled.
Light has no fellowship with darkness (1 John 1:5). As
Christians with the mind of Christ, we must ask of our
world, "Who are the oppressors and who are the
oppressed?" The Spirit of God may drive us into the
desert to sigh, cry, and pray for freedom for all humanity, into the arena of national or local politics to legis-

late it, into the marketplace to preserve it, into the bosom of our families to revitalize it, or into the heart of our own moribund churches to re-create it.

The unity so ardently desired and expressed by Jesus Christ in his high priestly prayer presupposes freedom in all its forms. The church as the visible body of the Lord is committed to achieving global freedom, to participating in the construction of a just social order, and to stimulating and radicalizing the dedication of Christians. The holy alliance between contemplation and action can revitalize the church's presence in the world and make its commitment to the Lordship of Jesus deeper and more radical.

As we come to possess the mind of Christ, we view our lives and growth in the Spirit quite simply. We know, to paraphrase Pascal, that all the liberation and revolution theologies, all the charismatic, Asiatic, and apophatic spiritualities, all the burial mounds of rhetoric and enfeebled good intentions, all the mumbling and fumbling of cerebral Christians busy cultivating their own idolatries, are not worth as much as one loving act that emancipates one slave from one moment of exile in Egypt.

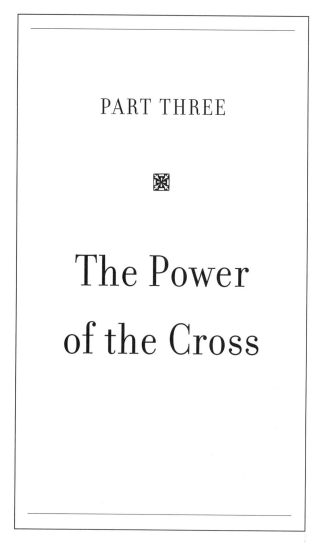

PART THREE

The Power
of the Cross

7.

Resurrection Wisdom

This examination of the mind of Christ is admittedly a simplified mental construct designed to locate, identify, and explore the complex web of desires, attitudes, motivations, thought patterns, and word games that motivate human behavior in the flesh and in the Spirit. It has as its goal transparency, which is inextricably tied to the Truth who is Jesus Christ. En route, the Holy Spirit jettisons the garbage in the junkyard of the mind, sweeps clean the attic of addictive emotional programming, frees the Christian from the damnable imprisonment of the flesh, and eliminates the considerable unnecessary suffering in life that is not born of the will of God. Now one crucial question remains: where does the transforming power lie? An exposition of the Christian life can be informative, even helpful, but "the kingdom of God is not a matter of talk but of power" (1 Corinthians 4:20).

No believer who is open to all that is true, just, lovely, gracious, and pure (Philippians 4:8) disdains the contributions of science. The study of psychology has added significantly to our understanding of human behavior and provided a key to unlocking the inner chambers of the mind. Many in the church have come to appreciate the emotional and spiritual benefits of counseling, meditation practices, yoga, contemplative prayer, and so forth. However, we must also recognize that these human activities remain limited in their ability to give us complete spiritual insight and direction. For that, we can only turn to the inspired Word of God. And the gospel points to only one source of redemption: the Cross of Jesus Christ.

Jesus Christ crucified is the power of God and the wisdom of God (1 Corinthians 1:24). The power of Pentecost flows from the Cross. Pentecost is not simply the feast of the Holy Spirit but the feast of the Resurrection power and glory of Jesus Christ communicated to others. Jesus could not be glorified until he had been crucified. Jesus was not constituted the messianic Son of God in power until he had died in the flesh. So it is with us. The power of the Risen Lord transmitted to the church through the Holy Spirit cannot be received except through participation in the death of Jesus.

For us, the death and resurrection process was initiated in conversion, but if we are to continue to drink of the life-giving water of the Spirit we must draw near to the body of our crucified God, from whom the saving waters flow (John 19:34). We must continually enter the "fellowship of sharing in his sufferings" (Philippians 3:10). If there are few Spirit-filled, power-laden, transparent Christians, it is because so few have plunged into the true life of Jesus and died to sin, selfishness, dishonesty, and degraded love. Whenever the Spirit of God blows like a hurricane through Christian history, it is through prophets and Christ lovers who have surrendered unconditionally to the folly of the Cross. "The mysteries of Christ's passion and dying," writes Bernard Tyrell, "are inexhaustibly rich in their healing meaning, value, and power."

The exploration of the mind of Christ is a journey to nowhere if the pilgrim is still handcuffed to the flesh. Transparency is obliterated if he draws a silk screen across the rough wood of the Cross. The power of the Spirit is dynamically operative only in those Christians who experience the fellowship of Jesus's suffering and the shame, humiliation, and pain of his Cross. Lucien

Cerfaux points out, "If the Word of the Cross is the power of God, it is precisely because it carries in itself the power of the Resurrection." The power of the Resurrection is nullified unless "we have crucified the sinful nature with its passions and desires" (Galatians 5:24). The impact of every serious effort at reform, renovation, and spiritual renewal in the United States will vanish like last night's dream if it is not sustained by the power of the paschal mystery. The unspeakable power of the Spirit is unleashed with astonishing force through the folly of the Cross—"a stumbling block to the Jews and foolishness to the Gentiles, but to those whom God has called, both Jews and Greeks, Christ the power of God and the wisdom of God. For the foolishness of God is wiser than man's wisdom, and the weakness of God is stronger than man's strength" (1 Corinthians 1:23–25).

For Paul, the perfect sign of human maturity is the Cross. It is the ultimate manifestation of the wholehearted love with which Jesus obeyed God's will amid the harsh realities of his earthly sojourn. The flame of filial love with which he ascended to his Father on Easter morning was the same love that had empowered him to endure the pain of his passion and death. Love was the meaning of the Cross even though its fire was hidden by shadows, and it was this same love that burst out of darkness into glory in the full radiance of the Resurrection. Barnabas Ahern writes:

*Because it is the same love that filled the heart of
the Crucified and lives in the risen Lord of glory,
one may wonder why Paul has not used the phrase,
"wisdom of the Resurrection." The answer is simple.
Paul wrote his epistles for people who lived in this
world and not in the world to come. To commend to
them "the wisdom of the Resurrection" would lack
the realism which the converts needed to face the
actuality of life upon earth. If the Corinthians were
foolish enough to think they had already entered upon
the fullness of the Risen Life (1 Corinthians 4:8),
this was the kind of fantasy Paul had to correct. Man
living in this world must face the harsh reality that
earthly life, seared by global and personal sin, can
never be Utopia.*

When Paul arrived at Corinth, he had just left Athens.
He was discouraged by his failure to win over the Greek
community there through his use of natural theology. In
speaking to the uncultured Corinthians, many of whom
led depraved lives, Paul completely abandoned the
wordy wisdom approach and preached the folly of the
Cross. "The message of the cross is foolishness to those
who are perishing, but to us who are being saved it is the
power of God" (1 Corinthians 1:18).

George Montague notes, "When Paul uses the word
foolishness or absurdity here, the Greek word (*moria*)
suggests something that is flat, dull, insipid—what is

foolish not in the sense of being publicly dangerous but rather publicly despised, ignored because it is ridiculous." And this is precisely what Paul proclaims. His words run counter to the natural taste of Jew and Greek, for he preaches Christ crucified. The Jews are indeed looking for a Messiah, but Jesus's shameful death on the Cross proves that he was not the glorious liberator they had awaited. The Cross remains a stumbling block to them, an obstacle to faith.

The Greeks envision the Messiah figure as a philosopher greater than Plato. He will lead men to contemplate the order and harmony of the universe. But a Messiah who will rattle this comfortable, cultured piety by reversing its values and going to his death on a cross, victim of the irrational dregs of humanity? Such a Messiah is indeed a stupidity to the Greeks.

Yet Paul preaches the folly of the Cross—the crucified Christ who is the power and wisdom of God—and he enjoys incredible success. The preaching of the Cross calls the Spirit to life. Jews and Greeks alike lay aside their prejudices to be swept up into the power and wisdom of the Cross.

Years later the church father John Chrysostom wrote:

*When those who seek signs and wisdom not only do
not receive the things they seek, but even hear the con-*

*trary to what they desire, and then by means of these
contraries are persuaded—does this not show the
unspeakable power of him who is preached? As if to
someone tempest-tossed and longing for a haven, you
were indeed to show not a haven but another wilder
portion of the sea, and yet he would follow you with
gratitude. Or as if a physician could attract to himself the man that was wounded and in need of medicine, by promising to cure him not with drugs, but by
burning him again! This is the result of great power
indeed. So also the Apostles won the day, not simply
without a sign, but even by a thing which seemed contrary to all the known signs.*

The whole Pauline canon suggests beyond any shadow of doubt that Paul is speaking here not only of the
Cross but of the Resurrection, which shows the former
to be the power of God and the wisdom of God. The
road map into the mind of Christ is emblazoned with
the sign of the Cross.

The four Gospels are the constituents of the early
church. They establish the basic character and essential
characteristics of the apostolic community. The modern church strives to conform to them. Whatever is
emphasized in the New Testament should be emphasized in the church today. Whatever is peripheral should
not be made central today. Jesus Christ in the mystery

of his death and resurrection is the center of the New Testament from Matthew's genealogy to Revelation's "Maranatha." In 1959 in an address at Venice, Italy, Giuseppe Montini put it this way: "To understand the paschal mystery is to understand Christianity; to be ignorant of the paschal mystery is to be ignorant of Christianity."

The same rigid logic must be applied to the spiritual life of the Christian. The church's spirituality is paschal spirituality and no other.

For a moment let us turn our attention again to Francis of Assisi, the man called by his contemporaries "the most perfect image of Christ that ever was." He climbed the holy mountain and his spirit serves as a torch up the narrow path. His biographer Thomas of Celano wrote: "Words only get in the way when one tries to express Francis' love for his crucified Lord." More than 130 years after the death of Francis, the theologian Bonaventure noted: "Love of Jesus Christ crucified so absorbed the mind of Francis that it revealed itself in his flesh. For two years before his death he bore in his body the brand marks of the Passion."

There are two surefire ways for Christians to deprive themselves of the power and wisdom of the Cross and therefore miss out on its transformative force. The first is to *intellectualize* the Passion, to speak in pedantic tones of the soteriological value of Jesus's redemptive death. This approach tones it down and wraps it up in a defensive cover that marks it for the mind only. There is no stirring in the rest of us—no pressure in the gut to change ourselves. The Cross is an ugly fact of our history, and we must resist the temptation to soften its meaning. Carlo Carretto says: "As Christians it is good for us not to boast of the Resurrection triumph without accepting the tremendous reality of [Christ's] crucifixion and death in us." We have softened the Cross by trivializing it (even to removing it in some of our churches), by fitting it neatly into our schematic theologizing, and by ignoring it in favor of the Resurrection.

The Passion of Jesus Christ did not take place on a cold, intellectual, starlit plane. We eviscerate its full meaning by speaking exclusively in the stained-glass tones of theological speculation. Even abstract sermons and effete homilies get in the way. Intellectualizing it is a subtle but effective way of robbing it of its power. Jurgen Moltmann quotes H. J. Iwand as saying, "We have made the bitterness of the cross, the revelation of God in the Cross of Jesus Christ, tolerable to ourselves by learning to understand it as a necessity for the process of salvation. . . . As a result the Cross loses its arbitrary and incomprehensible character."

The second way is to *mineralize* the Passion. You know that calm, familiar naked man hanging on a crucifix. By having turned him into a gold, silver, bronze, or marble object, we have freed ourselves from his agony and death as a man. "Isn't Dali's Christ of St. John of the Cross simply magnificent," we coo. Francis would have wept. The more we reproduce him, the more we forget about him and his third hour.

The day that the mineral man was crucified there was nothing to him but fear and flesh. Years ago a friend gave me a very expensive crucifix. A well-known contemporary artist had delicately carved the hands of Jesus into the wood. At the third hour, however, the Roman artists carved the crucified man with no art at all. No delicacy was needed to bang in the nails with hammers; no red pigment was needed to make a realistic trickle of blood flow from his hands and feet. His mouth was wonderfully contorted simply by hoisting him on the cross and leaving him there to quiver with pain.

We have so intellectualized and mineralized the passion of this sacred Man that we no longer see the slow unraveling of his tissue, the spread of gangrene, his raging thirst. Instead, our images of him seem so tranquil on our crucifixes, especially the ones that show him wearing priestly vestments. We assume from his quiet composure that his whole life was like that.

Jesus entered our world as the music man, but the world was disturbed by his song. On Good Friday the world went back to the peace it needed. Jesus wanted to turn the world into a great cathedral organ, and he dug music out of dry bread, herds of pigs, whores, and the dead. Nain, Jericho, Capernaum, and Bethany put two nails into his hands to silence his music. New York, Chicago, St. Louis, and Los Angeles do the same thing with their minds and their minerals.

I would like to be Saint Francis, if only for one hour. Not because the painter Renan called him "the only perfect Christian after Christ," not because the late Daniel Lord called him "the most Christlike of all the saints," and not because the theologian Romano Guardini said "Galilee returned to earth at Assisi." The secret of Francis's transparency is engrained in the wood of the Cross. He often fell into ecstasy before an image of his crucified Lord. In that one hour, the thoughts of Saint Francis would crack open all my tidy theological concepts and make me forget my beloved minerals. Security, pleasure, and power would cease their siren call because I would understand the mystery of the third hour and know the incomparable love in the heart of Jesus Christ that ravished his heavenly Father.

In the early days of the Franciscan Order, when the friars were unacquainted with the psalms, they asked Francis in great simplicity how they should pray. He answered, "Pray in this way—we adore you, Lord Jesus Christ, and we praise you, *because by your holy cross you have redeemed the world*." From his conversion to his death, Francis was preoccupied in both mind and heart with Jesus Christ crucified and the power and wisdom of God. The Cross was the cause of his poverty, the source of his perfect joy, the soul of his transparency. He was like a man obsessed, his mind aglow with one thought and his heart aflame with one desire—to know Christ crucified. Francis disengaged essentials from nonessentials and saw his way of life simply as an exterior consequence of an immense, passionate, and uncompromising love for the person of Jesus. To sign all his letters with the Tau, to make it the sole banner on the wall of his cell, to break with the monastic tradition of Benedict and found a mendicant order, to pass weeks and months in the Carceri (caves) in the gratuitous praise of God, to live in utter poverty and simplicity, were not desires for novelty but compulsions of love.

What is central in the New Testament must be central in the church's life today. What was central in Francis's life ought to be central in the life of the pilgrim seeking higher Christian understanding and transparent union with God.

I am writing these words at 2:00 a.m. on Good Friday morning. The campus of the university is asleep; my spirit is alive to God. Somewhere in the distance a radio is playing. It is an old spiritual, "I Believe in a Hill Called Mount Calvary." The words, "I believe that the Christ who was slain on the cross has the power to change lives today." I hear Jesus speaking the prophetic word in the stillness of the night:

"Little brother, perhaps the most difficult thing for you to accept at this moment is your failure to have done with your life what you long to accomplish. This is the cross you wanted least of all, the cross you never expected, the cross you find hardest to bear. Somewhere you got the idea that I expected your life to be an untarnished success story, an unbroken upward spiral toward holiness. Don't you see that I am too realistic for that?

"I witnessed a Peter who three times claimed that he did not know me, a James who wanted power in return for service to the kingdom, a Philip who after three years together didn't know he was supposed to see the Father in me, and a score of disciples who were sure I was finished on Calvary. The New Testament is full of men who started out well and faltered. Yet I appeared to Peter, and James is not remembered for his ambition but for his sacrifice of self for the kingdom. Philip did see the Father in Christ when I showed the way. And the disciples who despaired had enough courage to recognize me in the stranger at their side who broke bread with them in the gathering darkness at the end of the road to Emmaus. The point is this: I expect more failure from you than you expect from yourself.

"The most urgent thing for you now, little brother, is to desire to possess the Holy Spirit. Cry, sigh, and pray for the Spirit night and day in tireless intercession. The Spirit alone can drive you onward and upward. The Spirit alone can make you good and keep your eyes fixed on me.

"Happily, your life, like mine, looks beyond Calvary to Resurrection. And it is my human nature in its present risenness, shot through and through with the radiance of divinity, that shows like a brilliant mirror all that you are summoned to. If you have suffered with me, you will be glorified with me. The fate of Christ your brother is your fate. With the apostle Thomas go up to Jerusalem and die with me. As you go, do not fail to remember that when I ascended into heavenly places, I did not remove myself from earth. I left myself in many places and uniquely in your own heart. It is from your interior depths that you will draw strength to continue your journey, prizing nothing, valuing nothing, glorying in nothing save the cross that I carried on the long lonely road to Calvary."

The power and wisdom of God is singularly manifested in the death and resurrection of Jesus Christ. Is it really surprising that from Jesus's greatest act of love would flow his greatest power? The life of the Christian is not the imitation of a dead hero. The Christian lives in Christ, and Christ lives in the Christian through the Holy Spirit. We are empowered to live new lives where sin has no place. If we do not, we frustrate the power of the paschal mystery by our refusal of faith in the power. "How often are Christians unwilling to believe that they have been transformed and that the impossible has become possible?" asks John McKenzie.

Life in the Spirit

Without the Holy Spirit mediated through the Cross of Jesus, we are destined to lives of fear, addiction, and pain. But when we grasp the reality of the Cross and sublimate all to the will of the Holy Spirit, we tap into the rich vein of golden treasure available through the Spirit of God. Imagine life with these gifts:

THE GIFT OF EASTER: FREEDOM FROM THE FEAR OF DEATH

The death of Jesus qualifies the answer to the haunting and terrifying question of alienation and absurdity. We fear the end of life because it means the end of our influence, our affection, our time with those we love. The theologian Wolfhart Pannenberg writes:

> The death of Jesus has deprived death of its power to separate us from God. His death did not cut him off from God. Since the Father retains his communion

with Jesus in the latter's death on the Cross, death has
lost its power to detach from God. Consequently, fel-
lowship with God is open to all [people] whose life
has ended in death. God's love for the world is made
palpable in Jesus.

The promise of the paschal mystery is that there will be plenty of time—unending time—to know, love, and delight in one another in the kingdom of God.

THE GIFT OF DIETRICH BONHOEFFER: FORGIVING LOVE

"While we were still sinners, Christ died for us" (Romans 5:6). The incontrovertible sign of Christians who have experienced forgiveness is the ability to love their enemies. This is an extraordinary gift and the infallible mark of the activity of the Holy Spirit. "Love your enemies and do good to them. . . . Then your reward will be great, and you will be sons of the Most High, because he is kind to the ungrateful and wicked" (Luke 6:35).

We cannot possess the mind of Christ until we recognize ourselves as forgiven enemies of God and in like manner extend forgiveness and reconciliation to our own enemies. Jesus Christ crucified is not merely a heroic example to the church; he is the power of God, a living force transforming our lives through his Word: "Father, forgive them, for they do not know what they are doing" (Luke 23:34). In each act of personal for-giveness the Christian encounters the God Moses came to know: "And he passed in front of Moses proclaiming, 'The Lord, the Lord, the compassionate and gracious God, slow to anger, abounding in love and faithfulness, maintaining love to thousands, and forgiving wicked-ness, rebellion, and sin" (Exodus 34:6–7).

THE GIFT OF THE TAX COLLECTOR:
POVERTY OF SPIRIT

"He would not even look up to heaven, but beat his breast and said, 'God, have mercy on me, a sinner'" (Luke 18:13). The French poet Paul Claudel said that the greatest sin is to lose the sense of sin. The man without a lively sense of the horror of sin does not know Jesus Christ crucified. The knowledge that sin exists and that we are sinners comes only from the Cross. We can delude ourselves into believing that sin is simply an aberration or a lack of maturity; that pre-occupation with security, pleasure, and power is caused by oppressive social structures and personality quirks; that we are sinful but not sinners, since we are mere victims of circumstances, compulsions, environ-ment, addictions, upbringing, and so forth. The Passion nails these lies and rationalizations to the Cross of Truth. Even the last perversion of truth we cling to—the self-flattery that suggests we are being rather humble when we disclaim any resemblance to Jesus Christ—has to go when we stand face to face with the crucified Son of Man.

THE GIFT OF MOTHER TERESA: SELFLESS SERVICE

This gift embodies the mind of Christ. It is the most effective way of transcending the desires that continually focus attention on self. Mother Teresa dedicated herself to those whom most of us would cross the street to avoid—the dirty, the diseased, the infected, the desperate. Her motivation was not to gain recognition or even the good feeling of helping others. For Mother Teresa, service was about offering love, about giving away herself. She once said of her work, "It is not how much we do, but how much love we put in the doing. It is not how much we give, but how much love we put in the giving."

In his Passion, Jesus moves completely out of himself. He is the man for others. He forgets himself. He is concerned about his apostles (John 18:8). He tries to reach out to Pilate. He comforts the women on the way to the Cross. He pardons the good thief. He provides for the care of Mary and John as they stand at the foot of the Cross. The gift mediated here is the power to move out of oneself through selfless service.

THE GIFT OF FRANCIS OF ASSISI:
A JOYFUL HEART

"Dedicate yourselves to thankfulness" (Colossians 3:15). Thanksgiving is the song of the saved sinner. We have already seen that, steeped in Calvary-awareness of the merciful love of the redeeming God, the tenor of Francis's life became one of humble, joyful thanksgiving. Through no merit of our own but by divine mercy we have been called out of darkness into wondrous light. "For it is by grace you have been saved, through faith—and this not from yourselves; it is a gift of God" (Ephesians 2:8). The unnecessary emotional suffering connected with living by our desire for security, pleasure, and power—depression, anxiety, guilt, fear, and sadness—is vanquished by the transforming power of the love of Jesus Christ. The Cross is a confrontation with the overwhelming goodness of God and the mystery of his love. God is pleased when we work; he is delighted when we sing. And the saved sinner sings, "It is right to give him thanks and praise."

John J. English writes:

I remember the change in one person especially. A group of men who had known him for years were on retreat with this man and they could not get over the

way he changed. Even his facial expression was
transformed. All of a sudden he had become free.
The basic experience was the deep realization that
God loved him. It had been gained most through
prayer to our Lord hanging on the Cross. He was
deeply moved by Paul's words: "But God
demonstrated his own love for us in this: While we
were still sinners Christ died for us." His experience
of human love had not the power to free him as did
that simple prayer before the crucified Lord.

THE GIFT OF CHRIST CRUCIFIED:
FIDELITY TO ONE'S LIFE COMMITMENT

On Calvary, Jesus seals his election as Messiah, holds
firm to it despite the loneliness and desolation that are
exerting tremendous pressure against his self-awareness
as Son-Servant-Beloved. We participate in the pesach
(the Hebrew word for "breakthough") of Jesus by sharing in the suffering and dying that result from remain-
ing steadfast to our own commitment. The power of
darkness (security, pleasure, and power) attempts to
seduce us to turn back, to renege on our commitment,
to renounce our obedience to Christ by a kind of physical or moral self-annihilation. The Cross confronts us
with the cost of discipleship, reminds us that there is no
cheap Pentecost, and carries within it the living power
to enable us to endure the inevitable humiliations, rejec-

tions, sacrifices, and loneliness that the journey to higher Christian consciousness imposes.

THE GIFT OF MARY MAGDALENE: RECKLESS LOVE

In the realm of Christian discipleship, it is conceivable that the church has never had a greater lover of Jesus Christ than Mary Magdalene. The focus of her attention throughout the Passion was not suffering but the suffering Christ, "who loved her and delivered himself up for her." We must not allow these words to be interpreted as allegory. The love of Jesus Christ on the Cross was a burning reality for Magdalene, and her life is utterly incomprehensible without it. If you wish to speak of the Christian life, authentic spirituality, or the gifts of the Holy Spirit, you speak of Jesus Christ nailed to the Cross or you do not speak at all.

Commenting on the dinner in the home of Simon the Pharisee (Luke 7:36–50), Pere de la Columbiere said: "It is certain that of all those present the one who most honors the Lord is the sinner who is so persuaded of the infinite mercy of God that all her sins appear to her as but an atom in the presence of this mercy." Jesus said, "You will know the truth and the truth will set you free" (John 8:32). What is the basic truth that sets Mary Magdalene free? It is that God loves her with an overwhelming love. This gift, not the intellectual cognition but the experiential awareness of it, is mediated through the Spirit of Christ crucified. The personal living experience of the love of Jesus Christ is the power and the wisdom that illuminates, transforms, and transfigures Mary Magdalene and all the extravagant lovers in Christian history. The prophetic word of the Lord to Marjory Kempe of Lynn remains ever ancient, ever new: "More pleasing to me than all your prayers, penances, and good works is that you would believe that I love you."

Authentic Christianity

In the winter of 1968, I lived in a cave in the Zaragosa Desert in Spain. The cave, hewn out of the face of a granite mountain, was six thousand feet above the sea. There I never saw another human face or heard the sound of a human voice apart from Sunday mornings when a brother from the village of Farlete below brought food, drinking water, and kerosene for the lamp I used to read by at night. The cave was partitioned interiorly: on the right was a chapel with a striking stone altar, a tabernacle fashioned out of wrought iron and interlaced with red velvet that made it resemble a treasure chest, and a large crucifix on the rear wall. The left side of the cave was furnished with a stone slab that served as a bed, a stone desk, a wooden chair, a sterno stove, and a kerosene lamp. I got up each morning at two for what the ancient church called "nocturnal adoration."

On the night of December 13, 1968, in what began as a long and lonely hour of prayer, I heard Jesus say, "For love of you I left my Father's side. I came to you who ran from me, who fled me, who did not want to hear my name. For love of you I was covered with spit, punched and beaten, and fixed to the wood of the cross."

Just this morning in an hour of quiet time, I realized these words are still burned on my life. Whether I am in the state of sin or grace, fidelity or infidelity, the words remain. That night in 1968 I looked at the crucifix a long time and figuratively saw the blood streaming from every wound and pore in Christ's body. And I heard the cry of his blood: "This is not a joke. It is not a game or a laughing matter that I have loved you." The longer I looked the more I understood that no man has ever loved me and no woman could ever love me as he does. I learned that night what a wise Franciscan told me the day I entered the order: "Once you come to know the love of Jesus Christ, nothing else in the world will seem beautiful or desirable."

How long have you been a Christian? How long have you been living in the Spirit? Do you know what it is to love Jesus Christ? Do you know what it is to have your love unsatisfied, endured in loneliness, and ready to burst your restless, ravenous heart? Do you know what it is to have the pain taken away, the hole filled up, to reach out and embrace this sacred Man and say sincerely, "I cannot let you go. In good times and bad, victory and defeat, my life has no meaning without you." If this experience has not illuminated your life with its brilliance, then regardless of age, disposition, or state in life, you do not understand what it means to be a Christian.

This and this alone is authentic Christianity. Not a code of dos and don'ts, not a tedious moralizing, not a list of forbidding commandments, and certainly not the necessary minimum requirement for avoiding the pains of hell. Life in the Spirit is the thrill and the excitement of being loved by and falling in love with Jesus Christ. If the Spirit is not fire, it does not exist. The prayer that rises from my heart is this—if you haven't already, may you come to know in surpassing measure the incredible, passionate joy that I have known in the love of Jesus Christ crucified, the power of God, and the wisdom of God.

Epilogue

The Revolution

"The Lord said he wished me to be a fool, the like of which was never seen before," said Francis of Assisi. A gentle revolution will come through the little cadre of Christian fools who are willing to overthrow the established order by rearranging their lives around the mind of Christ. Their quest is transparency through truthfulness, and their lifestyles will be shaped by the gospel of Jesus Christ. If "truth consists in the mind's giving to things the importance they have in reality," in the words of Jean Daniélou, then the desire for security, pleasure, and power will be realistically assessed as straw and the Lordship of Jesus

Christ pragmatically affirmed as the order of the really Real.

The fools for Christ are violent, as the gospel enjoins them to be (Matthew 11:12), but the violence is done to themselves (Galatians 5:24). Their gentleness is the beautiful fruit of reverence for God, compassion for the world, and respect for themselves. Their priorities are personal, determined not by the popular religion of the day, by power politics, or by the consumer culture, but by the Sermon on the Mount and the paschal mystery. To the fool, Jesus Christ is not a sage or a starry-eyed reformer; he is the second Adam, author of a new creation: "I am making everything new!" (Revelation 21:5). He has redirected reality and given it a revolutionary reorientation. Jesus did not tidy up the world. He brought it to a screaming halt. What he refashioned out of the human stuff of the old order is not nicer people with better morals but brand-new creations (2 Corinthians 5:17).

The ranks of these revolutionaries transcend all class distinctions. Male versus female, priest versus layperson, progressive versus conservative, charismatic versus traditional, modern versus postmodern—all are dissolved in the unifying love of the Spirit (Galatians 3:28). The sole requirements for membership are the experiential awareness of Jesus as saving Lord and of God as Abba, unconditional surrender to the sway of the Holy Spirit, and stable commitment to the mission of building the new heavens and the new earth.

The sense of mission among the fools will create havoc in the neighborhood. Fears will be aroused, and rumors will circulate that these people are becoming "peculiar." Their friends will advise them to settle down and do something constructive with their lives (like seek out security, pleasure, or power). Neighbors will whisper that they are religious fanatics. Relatives will regale them with ostentatious displays of their dubious achievements. Each ploy will be designed to make them look and feel like what they actually are: fools. Catherine de Hueck Doherty says, "It seems as if the world needs fools—fools for Christ! Fools for God's sake! For it is such fools that have changed the face of the earth."

As they must (John 15:18), these fools will give offense. Today Christianity is largely inoffensive; this kind of religion will never transform anything. Jesus Christ the master revolutionary offended the religious and political order of Palestine. Christians too are bound to offend, and if we do not it is a bad sign—we cannot be very revolutionary.

Perhaps the revolution's leitmotiv, or controlling inspiration, can be best described through a dream I had while on a silent retreat in the wilderness. My spiritual director affirmed it as a faithful reflection of the gospel message and recommended that it be shared with God's people.

In my mind's eye, I see a man walking death row and a woman being readied for her lethal injection in a

Texas prison. I see the ovens at Auschwitz and Dachau and truckloads of dead Jewish bodies rolling into the night. I see Hiroshima and 95,000 burnt bodies, charred beyond recognition, littering the streets and hillsides. I see the crumpled body of John F. Kennedy overturned in death. I see Princess Diana lying in a closed casket in the cathedral in London.

Now I see rows of crosses outside the city wall of old Jerusalem with hundreds of bodies nailed to them—thieves, seditionists, murderers. On a hill I see three more crosses with the bodies of three more dead men, and they all look just the same, though the man in the middle seems to have been savaged and brutalized a bit more than the others.

Now it is two days later, and I find myself in the square of a large city. A bunch of men are running around as if they are crazy. They are saying the most preposterous thing: the crucifixion of the man on the middle of the three crosses was not just another political execution. They are saying that it is the most important event in the history of the world. They are saying that the man is now the focal point of faith and the object of worship for men of all ages for all time to come. They are beside themselves with joy. I am bewildered. This mad proclamation has no precedent in my study of world religions. It fits none of my theological categories. In terms of my religious understanding, it is a skandalon—an outrage. Besides, these men look a little spooky, and someone is saying that the woman with them used to be a hooker. Anyhow, he's dead. I saw him, and he was as dead as Kennedy lying in his casket. But just to make sure, I return to that hillside. As I stand there staring up at what is now an empty cross, a man steps over the rim of the horizon. From somewhere a mighty chorus is singing, "King of Kings and Lord of Lords."

I look around. I am no longer alone. As far as the eye can see, the landscape is dotted with people. They are all singing "King of Kings and Lord of Lords." The man comes striding into focus. He is bathed in light. As if two curtains are being drawn aside, the skies open and are filled with the most beautiful beings I have ever seen. The man stops and raises his hand. The earth falls silent. I look at the man. His face is aglow like a sunburst at dawn, his eyes are brilliant like two North Stars. "Peace be to you," he says. His words are more a command than a greeting. The universe sinks into deeper stillness.

"Come to me," he says, "as I call you by your name. Yes, I know your name. I knew you when you were awake and asleep. Before a word was on the tip of your tongue, I knew the whole of it. I scrutinized your every movement. With all your ways I am familiar. More than a shepherd knows his sheep do I know you by name. Come to me."

The roll call begins. I see Bob Dylan and Bono; Francis of Assisi steps forward, followed by Martin

Luther. I see Howard Hughes and Dorothy Day, Adolph Hitler and Mohandas Gandhi, Nelson Rockefeller and Charles de Foucauld. Following them are Saint Augustine and Ray Charles, the prophet Amos and Hugh Hefner, Jeremiah and David Letterman, Mary and Joseph, Paris Hilton and Brad Pitt, Peter, James, and John. Kim Jong-il and George W. Bush. There's my brother, my neighbor, the guy who tried to wash my windshield on the streets of New York. On and on they go. All the beautiful, famous, and powerful people and the billions of unfamous, unsung, uncelebrated ones.

I hear my name called—"Brennan." As I step forward, the man looks at me, then through me. He looks through all my bluff and rhetoric, through my books and retreats, beyond all my rationalizing, minimizing, and justifying. For the first time I am seen and known as I really am.

Trembling, I ask, "What is my judgment, Lord?"

He answers firmly but gently, "I am not your judge." He hands me the Book. "The word I spoke has already judged you."

A long pause . . . then he smiles. I walk up to him and touch his face. He takes my hand and we go home.

The content of this dream is more real than the book you are holding in your hand. At an exact day and hour known only to the Father (Matthew 24:36), Jesus Christ, the King of Glory, will upstage all the beautiful, famous, and powerful people who have ever lived.

Every man and woman who has ever drawn breath will be appraised, evaluated, and measured solely in terms of their relationship with the Carpenter from Nazareth. This is the realm of the really Real. The Lordship of Jesus Christ and his primacy in the created order (Ephesians 1:10) are at the center of the gospel proclamation. This is reality.

When the fools who seek to live with the mind of Christ ask themselves, "Why do I exist?" they answer, "For the sake of Jesus Christ." If the angels ask, it is the same answer: "For the sake of Jesus Christ." If the whole universe were suddenly to become articulate, from north to south and from east to west it would cry out in chorus, "We exist for the sake of Christ." The name of Jesus would issue from the seas and mountains and valleys; it would be tapped out by the pattering rain. It would be written with lightning in the skies. The storms would roar the name "Lord Jesus Christ God-hero," and the mountains would echo it back. The sun on its westward march through the heavens would chant a thunderous hymn, "The whole universe is full of Christ."

If there is any priority in our personal or professional lives more important than the Lordship of Jesus Christ, we disqualify ourselves as witnesses to the gospel and from membership in the gentle revolution. Since the day when Jesus burst the bonds of death and the messianic era erupted into history, there is a new agenda, a unique set of priorities, and a revolutionary hierarchy of values for the believer. The Carpenter did not simply refine Platonic or Aristotelian ethics, reorder Old Testament spirituality, or renovate the old creation. He brought a revolution. We must renounce all that we possess, not just most of it. We must give up our old way of life, not merely correct some slight aberrations in it. We are to be an altogether new creation, not simply a refurbished version of it. We are to be transformed from one glory to another, even into the very image of the Lord—transparent. Our minds are to be renewed by a spiritual revolution.

The primal sin, of course, is to go on acting as if it never happened. When we are hungry for God, we move and act, become alive and responsive; when we are not, we are dilettantes playing spiritual games. "God is of no importance unless He is of supreme importance," said Abraham Heschel. An intense inner desire to learn to think like Jesus is already the sign of God's presence. The rest is the operation and activity of the Holy Spirit.

I suppose most of us are in the same position as the Greeks who approached Philip and said, "We would like to see Jesus" (John 12:21). The only question is: "How badly?"